Prognosis: Fair

A TRAUMA CASE STUDY FOR CLINICIANS

FRANCES SOUTHWICK, DO

Do not ignore the pain.
Give it purpose.

—Amanda Gorman,
"The Miracle of Morning"

CONTENTS

FRONT MATTER

PLAYLIST

For an enhanced reading experience, consider purchasing the songs in this playlist. Prompts sprinkled throughout the text indicate when to play each song. The QR code[1] above links to the *Prognosis: Fair* playlist on Spotify (which includes most of these songs).

1. "Dark Road" by Annie Lennox

2. "Going Down" by Ani DiFranco

3. "Studying Stones" by Ani DiFranco

4. "Can't Buy Me Love" by the Beatles

5. "Love Me Like You Hate Me" by Rainsford

6. "Natural Law" by Frazey Ford

---

1 Focus your phone's camera on the QR code as if to snap a photo, then tap the pop-up message.

7.   "Weather Pattern" by Frazey Ford

8.   "Revolutionary Love" by Ani DiFranco

9.   "One Voice" by The Wailin' Jennys

10. "45" by Judith Avers

11. "You Don't Know" by Brooke Annibale

12. "Wise Up" by Aimee Mann

13. "Winter Coat" by Karen Savoca[2]

14. "Heaven's Here on Earth" by Tracy Chapman

15. "First Aid Kit" by Judith Avers and Joanna Burt-Kinderman

16. "Fireflies" by Judith Avers

---

2 Available on Bandcamp and iTunes, but not on Spotify.

READ THIS FIRST

Prognosis: Fair is a book about trauma. Care has been taken to reduce the risk of secondary trauma for the reader via the removal of graphic descriptions, slurs, and intimidating language. Throughout the book, bracketed text substitutes for graphic depictions. Nevertheless, this book still contains some references to abuse, suicidal thoughts and behaviors, and children witnessing domestic violence.[3]

This book projects a collage of the pieces of my life through a trauma-focused lens. It does not represent my life as a whole, nor all the people in it, nor my entire trauma narrative. I used the literary non-fiction style so as to emotionally engage the reader in a vivid, human-ized experience of the events discussed. This book was written in good faith with the principle aim of helping health care providers understand the inherent unity of neurology and psychology via examination of the effects of trauma and its processing.

If you suspect, know of, or vehemently deny the presence of unre-solved trauma in your life, then please contact a psychotherapist and engage in treatment (including stabilization, crisis planning, and social support) before reading this book. If you live with traumatic memories, then please consider having a consultation with a psychotherapist before

---

3 The appendices of *Prognosis: Fair*, which form the last quarter of the book, include helpful coping strategies and support documents to foster stability during and after trauma processing. If you are hesitant about reading potentially traumatizing material, then you may consider skipping ahead to this section.

engaging with this text, even if you have been in therapy for years. Thank you for your self-reflection.

Some names and identifying characteristics have been changed for the privacy of those depicted in the text. I relied on my own memory and on public documents for the content of this book, and some dialogue has been reconstructed to help convey key concepts.

This book is sold with the understanding that the author and publisher are not engaged in rendering medical, health, or any other kind of professional services via the book. The reader should consult a medical, behavioral health, or other trusted professional before adopting any of the suggestions in the book or drawing inferences from the book.

For further exploration of the post-traumatic stress disorder spectrum, I suggest keeping a few texts handy while reading this book: (1) *Trauma and Recovery* by Judith Herman, (2) both volumes of *The Body Remembers* by Babette Rothschild, and (3) *The Body Keeps the Score* by Bessel van der Kolk.

NOTE ON RACE

Arisika Razak, professor emerita of the graduate program in women's spirituality at the California Institute of Integral Studies and core teacher at the East Bay Meditation Center in Oakland, California, writes about the trauma of racial oppression:

> Trauma, by definition, attacks the individual's coping skills and threatens the organism's stability. It has been with us since humanity's beginnings as we experience death, illness, loss, and environmental catastrophe. However, sociocultural oppression enacts a burden that is in addition to the normal traumas of life. (2021)

I am white and live in the United States. I am not on the receiving end of racial oppression. If I was, my life would look a lot different, and I doubt I would have the energy, space, and time to write a book like this. I honor and strive to learn more about the trauma of people of color, and I aspire to make anti-racist thought and behavior changes in my life and use my privilege to share my experience as mindfully as I can.

Those cited in *Prognosis: Fair* and the editors of the text are racially diverse. This effort has enriched the text immensely. I call on other authors to consider the racial diversity of those they read, cite, and employ.

ACKNOWLEDGMENTS

Thank you to the developers and editors of this book, including Helene Alphonso, Judith Avers, the Davis Writer's Salon, Emma Eisenberg, Rebecca Jo Hoss, T. J. Hurt, Ian Kim, Carolyn Levin, the Madwomen in the Attic at Carlow University, Cynthia Magistro, Babette Rothschild, Tomoko Sairenji, and Lauryn Smith du Toit.

I also extend thanks to each person and organization that helped in my recovery (directly or indirectly), especially Judith Avers, Michael Avers, Allyson Baber, Sandra L. Bloom, Taffie Bucci, Tarana Burke, Vincent Chiu, Andrea Constand, Mustang Sally Cooper, Judge K. D., Ani DiFranco, Allyson Dinneen, James Dodge, Dreams of Hope, Isabel Edge, Suzanne Emam, Faith, Farin, Frazey Ford, Viktor E. Frankl, Greg Gallik, Martha Gilmore, Emily Hall, Johann Hari, Judith Herman, Kimberly Hinton, Suska Holtzman, Becky Jo Hoss, I. K., Det. M. K., N. K., Ian Kim, Nancy Kirkwood, James Kribs, Connie Lappa, Casper Leung, Marsha Linehan, the Madwomen in the Attic at Carlow University, Cynthia Magistro, Nancy Malecki, Melissa Malone, Melissa Marshall, Men Can Stop Rape, Rebecca Mertz, Betsy Meux, Gloria Miele, Andrea Nazar, Sgt. O., Beverly Ogilvie, Peggy Ott, Det. N. P., Jessica Perea, Phil Phelps, Christina Poppito, Stephen Porges, Mr. Rainer, Aubrey Raney-Avers, Erika Roshanravan, Tomoko Sairenji, Karen Savoca, Marilyn Sherwin, Pat Stewart, A. T. Still, Todd Swallows, and W. W. My sincerest apologies to those whose names have been omitted.

The specific works of many others have also fostered my recovery, including, but not limited to, Tarana Burke's revolutionary #MeToo movement, the late Jean Baker Miller's ability to call a spade a spade in the book *Toward a New Psychology of Women*, Peter Levine's description of the body's instinctual trembling response to heal trauma in the book *In an Unspoken Voice*, Babette Rothschild's "Window of Affect Tolerance and Integration" in the second volume of *The Body Remembers*, Stanley Rosenberg's explanation of the polyvagal/cranial nerve and related exercises in the book *Accessing the Healing Power of the Vagus Nerve*, Bessel van der Kolk's practical and non-traumatizing physical approach taught through the Complex Trauma Treatment Network, Rebekah Ballagh's "Journey to Wellness" illustrations, Carlow University's Madwomen in the Attic's nonfiction writing courses (led by Nancy Kirkwood), Johann Hari's TED talks on addiction and depression, Allyson Dinneen's book *Notes from Your Therapist*, Ani DiFranco's kaleidoscopic catalog of music (especially the pieces "The Slant" and "Going Down," as well as her album *Revolutionary Love*) and her book *No Walls and the Recurring Dream*, Aimee Mann's music (especially the song "Wise Up"), Frazey Ford's album *Indian Ocean*, and Karen Savoca's album *Figure it Out*.

An extra special thank you goes to my day-in, day-out bastions: my wife, Judith Avers, and my sister, Becky Jo Hoss.

Finally, my thanks go to you, the reader. Thank you for choosing this book. I hope it helps you and those you know and serve.

DEFINITIONS
AND ABBREVIATIONS

Child maltreatment: A harmful and potentially traumatizing environment, relationship, or behavior inflicted upon a child by an abuser, either by commission (abuse) or omission (neglect).

Child sexual abuse (CSA): A form of child abuse wherein a child is coerced or forced into (contact or noncontact) sexualized experiences. (Definition adapted from the Rape, Abuse & Incest National Network [n.d.] and the World Health Organization [1999].)

Complex post-traumatic stress disorder (c-PTSD): An acquired disorder with onset after repeated, prolonged, totalitarian control-type trauma. It is evidenced by alterations in affect regulation, consciousness, self-perception, perception of the perpetrator, relations with others, and systems of meaning. Examples of individuals who may have c-PTSD include hostages, prisoners of war, survivors of concentration camps, survivors of some religious cults, and those involved in totalitarian systems in sexual and domestic life, including those subjected to domestic battering, childhood physical or sexual abuse, and organized sexual exploitation. (Definition adapted from Judith Herman [1997].)

Developmental trauma disorder (DTD): An acquired disorder in children and adolescents that often carries into adulthood. It is evidenced by the triggered pattern of repeated dysregulation in response to trauma cues wherein changes persist and do not return to baseline, cause functional impairment, and are not reduced in intensity by conscious awareness. It is characterized by persistently altered attributions and expectancies of the self, others, relationships, and society, and it follows multiple exposures or chronic exposure to one or more forms of developmentally adverse interpersonal trauma, such as abandonment, betrayal, physical assault, sexual assault, threats to bodily integrity, coercive practices, emotional abuse, and witnessing violence or death. (Definition adapted from Bessel van der Kolk [2015].)

Dissociation: A neuropsychiatric self-protecting mechanism employed to dull the experience of and thus survive traumatic events (initially involuntarily, but it may be honed for voluntary use). It is evidenced by compartmentalization of parts of an experience. For example, one may be able to intellectually describe an event but not sense the emotions, or one may recall a memory from a location other than one's own body. (Definition adapted from Richard J. Loewenstein [2018].)

Neuropsychosocial: Denotes the dynamic, inseparable interplay of the neuropsychological and social facets of the self.

Post-traumatic stress disorder (PTSD): An acquired disorder with onset after an experience of trauma[4] (direct or witnessed) that creates distress or functional impairment for at least one month. It is characterized by repeatedly reliving elements of the traumatic experience (via involuntary or voluntary rumination and/or consciously or subconsciously driven behavioral reconstruction or repetition), avoidance of reminders of the trauma, negative thoughts or feelings, and heightened neuropsychiatric arousal. (Definition adapted from the American Psychiatric Association [2013].)

---

4 In the fifth edition of the *Diagnostic and Statistical Manual of Mental Disorders (DSM-5)*, the American Psychological Association (2013) names specific traumatic experiences as requisite for the diagnosis of PTSD: death, threatened death, actual or threatened serious injury, or actual or threatened sexual violence. I interpret "injury" to include physical, moral, and/or neuropsychosocial injury.

Self: An individual human being; a unified body and psyche; an inherently social, sensing, thinking, feeling, believing, knowing, behaving clump of intricately organized and energized matter.

Trauma: Lasting injury to the self.[5]

Traumatic brain injury (TBI): An acquired disorder with onset after brain trauma. It is characterized by disordered neuropsychological functioning. It is evidenced by at least one neuropsychological sign or symptom, such as loss of consciousness; headache; confusion; light-headedness; dizziness; cranial nerve dysfunction; fatigue; lethargy; changes in sleep patterns; behavioral or mood changes; trouble with memory, concentration, attention, or thinking; nausea; vomiting; convulsions; seizures; inability to awaken from sleep; dilation of one or both pupils; slurred speech; weakness or numbness in the extremities; loss of coordination; restlessness; and agitation. Symptoms may be mild, moderate, or severe, depending on the extent of damage to the brain. (Definition adapted from the National Institute of Neurological Disorders and Stroke [2019].)

---

5 Many definitions of trauma exist. This "shortcut" definition allows one to hold the core meaning of trauma while digesting other pieces of information about trauma. The severity, quality, and duration of injury depend on many factors, including the person's age when the trauma took place, the coping resources available to the person at the time of injury, the nature of the relationship between the injured party and the source of injury, the responses of the person's family and first confidante, and more.

THE PATIENT PRESENTS

INTRODUCTION

Public truth-telling is the common denominator of all social action.

—Judith Herman, *Trauma and Recovery*

Musical Introduction: "Dark Road" by Annie Lennox

Our stories are ours, to share or to hold. This book is a case study of myself, and after much deliberation and therapy,[6] I have decided to share my story since there is nothing like a case study when it comes to learning new material.

In my first book, *Prognosis: Poor*, I detailed some of my experiences from my training to become a family doctor. Its primary aims were to provide validation, curry solidarity, and expand understanding and empathy for medical trainees and their loved ones.

---

6 I have read trauma literature. I have also employed several therapists, and spoken with many more as colleagues. In addition, I have completed ten weeks of an intensive outpatient program founded on dialectical behavioral therapy (DBT), as well as several sessions of eye movement and desensitization reprocessing (EMDR). (It should be noted that EMDR has been found to be "sensationally effective" for one-time trauma but less effective for syndromes following more complex, pervasive trauma [van der Kolk 2015].) Moreover, I have interviewed people who knew of and/or witnessed the events described in this book.

Prognosis: Fair also draws on my past. As with *Prognosis: Poor*, this book is not my catharsis, but a learning tool. My goal is to offer medical providers and behavioral health clinicians a deeper cognitive and visceral understanding of trauma processing. I do this by illustrating the story of a traumatized person with an educational background in philosophy and medicine (and gradually trauma), and by peppering in quotes and data from artists, authors, and trauma researchers and clinicians.

"Everything we therapists do or say or feel as we sit with our patients is mediated by our histories; everything I've experienced will influence how I am in any given session at any given hour."
—Lori Gottlieb, *Maybe You Should Talk to Someone*

All of us (including therapists and other medical providers) are shaped by our experiences, and our behaviors are based on those experiences. As our behaviors directly impact patient care, we owe it to our clients and patients to dive in and understand ourselves.

I am sharing my story with you because the process of integrating my traumatic experiences into my current life has yielded such great gains, both personally and professionally.[7]

. . .

In November 2014, when the news was aflame with survivors speaking out about Bill Cosby's abuses, my own trauma history sparked

---

7 *Prognosis: Fair* focuses on my processing of my personal trauma. Processing my trauma has markedly improved my clinical skills and ability to connect with patients, but patients' stories and my clinical experiences as a physician are beyond the scope of this book.

back to life.[8] I quickly found myself in the thick of reexperiencing prior traumas. To cope, I referenced medical literature for self-education, but the standard definitions and explanations of PTSD did not explain the engulfment I was experiencing. I began treatment with a therapist that same month. My wife, Judith, was already working with a psychologist who strongly recommended Judith Herman's book *Trauma and Recovery: The Aftermath of Violence—From Domestic Abuse to Political Terror.*[9] This book named and narrated parts of my life with uncanny precision and served as my Rosetta Stone for processing trauma.

Herman notes the importance of context when it comes to trauma. It is not only the traumatic event and initial response that matter; when considering the whole picture of a traumatic event, the circumstances leading up to and following the incident are just as relevant (Herman 1997).

There is a constellation of potential post-traumatic life experiences and feelings, including survivorship, victimization, dissociation, abuse perpetuation, and suicide. The survivor's post-traumatic landscape depends on their preexisting coping strategies and capacity, their social capital (the value of the tangible and intangible resources within their proximate social network), the responses of those in their network, and the resources available to them.

---

8 The more vigorously the sympathetic and/or dorsal vagal portions of the autonomic nervous system (fright, fight, flight, freeze, collapse) are activated during an experience, the more pervasively the organism's brain and behaviors are altered. The pieces of a traumatic event may include involuntarily selected thoughts, beliefs, emotions, sensations, images, and behaviors. Some of these pieces may be experienced or expressed at or near the time of the event, while others may lie dormant. The dormant pieces may be reactivated later in life by triggering events.

9 *Trauma and Recovery* is the most worn and annotated book on my shelf.

True to its full title, *Trauma and Recovery* compares the two most common categories of life-altering c-PTSD:[10] domestic terror (neuro-psychological, emotional, and sexual abuse dealt by men to women and girls in their homes) and political terror (post-war syndromes). *Prognosis: Fair* personifies domestic-abuse-driven c-PTSD and stretches the paradigm to include two outliers: a young abuser[11] and a female abuser.[12]

...

Lewisburg, West Virginia. 2006. Second year of medical school.

I sat at attention in a lecture on emotional health, willing my brain to grasp the concept.

"Emotions are physical," said the lecturer.

Those in the room responded to her statement with smirks and side-eyes, even the course director who sat beside me in the audience. The lecturer pressed on.

---

10 Herman developed the diagnostic criteria for c-PTSD as a means to recognize, diagnose, and understand the lives and behaviors of those who have experienced prolonged, repeated trauma. She explains the need for the diagnostic label: "Even the diagnosis of 'post-traumatic stress disorder,' as it is presently defined, does not fit accurately enough. The existing diagnostic criteria for this disorder are derived mainly from survivors of circumscribed traumatic events. They are based on the prototypes of combat, disaster and rape. In survivors of prolonged, repeated trauma, the symptom picture is often far more complex. Survivors of prolonged abuse develop characteristic personality changes, including deformations of relatedness and identity. Survivors of abuse in childhood develop similar problems with relationships and identity; in addition, they are particularly vulnerable to repeated harm, both self-inflicted and at the hands of others. The current formulation of post-traumatic stress disorder fails to capture either the protean symptomatic manifestations of prolonged, repeated trauma or the profound deformations of personality that occur in captivity" (1997).

11 A study of forty-seven child perpetrators showed that perpetrators can start offending at age four, and in all cases studied, the child perpetrators used coercion (Johnson 1988).

12 If this is a novel concept for the reader, consider referencing Beverly Ogilvie's (2004) study of sixty adult female survivors of sexual abuse from their mothers.

"Think of what happens when you get embarrassed. Your shoulders shrug, your head cocks downward, you blush. That's a *physical reaction* due to an *emotion*."

Until that moment, despite my interest in theories involving the mind-body connection, I had believed that emotions were optional and separate from the physical self. Synapses, neurotransmitters, carbon, fluid, and so on were how I understood the brain and body. For me, the mind and emotions were floating, enigmatic, maybe even invented concepts.

...

As a physician I prescribe medications for pain, seizures, bipolar disorder, depression, anxiety, insomnia, and many other conditions. What is interesting to me is the overlap. For example, some medications for seizures are also effective for bipolar disorder (e.g., valproic acid, lamotrigine, carbamazepine), and some medications for nerve pain are also helpful for depression, anxiety, and/or insomnia (e.g., gabapentin, duloxetine, nortriptyline).

In all these cases (seizures, depression, nerve pain, bipolar disorder, etc.), we are describing and treating altered functioning of the same parts of the self: neurons and synapses. The central processing unit. The brain. The mind.

Neurology is psychology. Not metaphorically, but literally. Like Clark Kent/Superman or Hannah Montana/Miley Cyrus, the brain and mind are heads and tails of one indivisible coin (Damasio 2005; Still 1899; Pert 1997).

For many diagnosticians, neuropsychological changes related to contact injury are easier to conceptualize than those related to noncontact injury; we accept the tangible and visible as real. However, just as contact trauma (e.g., blunt force, contrecoup) causes brain/mind (neuropsychological) injury, so do biochemical, metabolic, and psychosocial noncontact traumas (e.g., vitamin B12 deficiency, autoimmune demyelination, lead toxicity, verbal and sexual abuse).

The bottom line is that it may improve patient care to lump traditionally labeled "neurological" and "psychological" phenomena under one overarching "neuropsychological" heading. Currently, one label is regarded as standard medicine while the other is regarded as optionally covered when it comes to health insurance. But these terms are simply two labels for a single organ system's behavior. Specialists in the nervous system could thus be trained and titled not as psychiatrists or neurologists, but as neuropsychiatrists.

My Neuropsychological Symptoms and Diagnoses Through The Years	
Age	Symptoms and Diagnoses
Elementary School (4–11 Years)	Symptoms: Onset of functional abdominal pain; dizziness; and intermittent suicidal ideation
Junior High (12–14 Years)	Symptoms: Onset of cataplexy; derealization; and intermittent self-injurious behavior
High School (14–17 Years)	Symptoms: Onset of excessive daytime sleepiness; pelvic pain; restrictive eating; and ritualistic binge-purge behavior
College (17–21 Years)	Diagnosis: Bulimia nervosa
Medical Training (21–29 Years)	Symptoms: Onset of episodes of persistent suicidal ideation; unilateral ptosis with dysesthesia of the right side of the face and right arm, which worsened with stress and poor sleep Diagnosis: Major depressive disorder
Post-Residency (30+ Years)	Symptoms: Onset of episodes of sleep paralysis and flashbacks; suicidal behavior, which led to a five-day psychiatric hospitalization, with completion of a ten-week intensive outpatient program Diagnoses: PTSD; migraine with aura; narcolepsy with cataplexy

TRAUMA IN CHILDREN

According to the Division of Violence Prevention of the National Center for Injury Prevention and Control, a division of the Centers for Disease Control and Prevention, "Toxic stress during childhood can harm the most basic levels of the nervous, endocrine, and immune systems, and . . . can even alter the physical structure of DNA (epigenetic effects)" (2019).

In other words, **"What you do to children matters. And they might never forget"** (Morrison 2015).

Maltreatment of children is sadly prevalent. Some argue it is the largest public health problem in the United States (van der Kolk 2015). In 2019 homicide was the No. 3 cause of death in the United States for age groups 1–4 years, 5–9 years, and 10–14 years, and it was the No. 2 cause of death for those aged 15–24 years (Centers for Disease Control and Prevention 2021).

Regarding child abuse from primary caregivers, Judith Herman writes:

> Repeated trauma in adult life erodes the structure of the
> personality already formed, but repeated trauma in childhood
> forms and deforms the personality. . . . She perceives daily,
> not only that the most powerful adult in her intimate world is
> dangerous to her, but also that the other adults who are respon-
> sible for her care do not protect her. . . . The child feels that she
> has been abandoned to her fate. . . . She must find a way to form
> primary attachments to caretakers who are either dangerous or,
> from her perspective, negligent. . . . To preserve her faith in her

parents, she must reject the first and most obvious conclusion that something is terribly wrong with them. She will go to any lengths to construct an explanation for her fate that absolves her parents of all blame and responsibility. (1997)

The term "child abuse" usually conjures images of bruised, beaten children. However, physical non-accidental trauma from a caregiver to a child is often the tip of a domestic terror iceberg. A child's trust and fear are easily engaged (i.e., they are implicit in the caregiver-child relationship), and injury does not require beatings. The fear a child endures due to abuse is enough to cause neuropsychosocial damage, and the dissociation the child must use to survive may mask the severity of dysfunction.

Kids suffering from sexual abuse rarely show physical signs (save behavior changes, which are often subtle).[13] This type of abuse is so insidious, the victim may not even sense there is a problem because attention and love shown to a child in the form of grooming (increasingly intimate exchanges, often beginning with seemingly innocuous kind comments, praise, or gifts) can lead seamlessly to sexual abuse. For the abuser, the ambiguity of that elusive seam and the absence of photographable evidence of the abuse enables manipulation, confusion, and discreditation of the child.

Oprah Winfrey had an aha moment related to child abuse, or as she astutely calls it, the "seduction of children":

It wasn't until many years later on a show with child molesters, one of them shared how they calculate and artfully manipulate

---

13 I reflect on the phrase "kids are resilient" and wonder if the subtext is that kids' well-being can be ignored and neglected because they have no power and will almost certainly survive. As Bessel van der Kolk says, "Children have a biological instinct to attach—they have no choice. Whether their parents or caregivers are loving and caring or distant, insensitive, rejecting, or abusive, children will develop a coping style based on their attempt to get at least some of their needs met" (2015).

to seduce children, when I finally realized, like so many of you, it really wasn't my fault. (Oprah.com, 2011)

For some perpetrators, child sexual abuse is indeed a calculated crime. Yet for other abusers, it is either a covert bleeding of boundaries as a means of conscious self-comfort or self-gratification, or it is a subconsciously driven compulsion. The perpetrator may blindly mimic their past instead of labeling and healing their post-traumatic wounds. Put differently, when we do not have words, we use actions (C. Magistro, pers. comm., 2014).

We know that child sexual abuse causes devastating and sometimes psyche-shattering fallout, both at the time of the abuse and later in the victim's life. Even though the abuser's intent may not be malicious, every action has a reaction (Newton 1686).

...

"My Instructors in science and technology have taught us about how the brain works," Jonas told him eagerly. "It's full of electrical impulses. It's like a computer. If you stimulate one part of the brain with an electrode, it—" He stopped talking. He could see an odd look on The Giver's face.

"They know nothing," The Giver said bitterly. . . .

"Nothing?" Jonas whispered nervously. "But my instructors—"

The Giver flicked his hand as if brushing something aside. "Oh, your instructors are well trained. They know their scientific facts. Everyone is well trained for his job.

"It's just that . . . without the memories it's all meaningless."

—Lois Lowry, *The Giver*

THE HOUSE, PART 1

Whose house is this? Whose night keeps out the light in here?
Say, who owns this house? It's not mine. I dreamed another, sweeter,
brighter with a view of lakes crossed in painted boats; of fields wide
as arms open for me. This house is strange. Its shadows lie.
Say, tell me, why does its lock fit my key?

—Toni Morrison, *Home*

My room is cold.

You can't see it, but the walls are filled with black syrupy material instead of pink fluffy insulation. It's liquid with dead things in it,
rotting. Burglars kept stealing my things and leaving soppy bags of this
material behind. I had to store it someplace . . . couldn't let anyone see
me taking it out with the regular trash. They can't know the room has
been robbed; we must preserve the neighborhood image. So I decided to
hide it. Standing on a small ladder in my bedroom, I carefully tapped a
hole into the top of the wall and funneled it in when no one was watching. The cold dark liquid is full of slimy dead things. I don't even know
what they are. But I know this room is worthless.

Month by month, millimeter by millimeter, the sludge soaked the
drywall, and eventually cracked the paint . . .

PAINT CRACKING

If you avoid the conflict to keep the peace,
you start a war inside yourself.

—C. Richardson, pers. comm., n.d.

"I feel sorry for Bill Cosby," Carrie said.

She had been working as staff in our office for over a year, but she still looked too young to be wearing scrubs.

My abdominal diaphragm spasmed. I instantly felt physically sick.

"Are you kidding me?!" I retorted without thinking, then quickly reprimanded myself.

Frances, calm down. Remember, she sees you as Dr. Southwick.

Her eyes shot down to her clipboard full of vital signs, and her body slumped away from me. But she held her ground.

"I mean, how do you know those girls aren't makin' it up?" she asked.

Now I was really nauseated. The right side of my face was tingling. I opened my mouth again to reply but was dumb.

A call came from the front desk.

"Chart's up, Southwick."

Carrie excused herself and shrank away to greet the next patient. I took a sip of water.

Why am I so upset? I don't even know Cosby.

It was November 2014, and I was in my second year of practice, working as a family physician in Pittsburgh, Pennsylvania. The serial rape allegations against Bill Cosby had just erupted.

I was disgusted by him. I felt betrayed by a childhood idol. With every woman who bravely presented a new allegation, I became more depressed and terrified, and I could not stop the tsunami of revulsion. I dry heaved in the mornings and breathed through anxiety attacks in the afternoons.

Bumping along Braddock Avenue in my red Honda Fit after work that day, my imagination returned to its recurrent visions of [suicidal ideation]. I reached my street, parked, walked into our home, and set my work bag and stethoscope down. I walked short, slow steps into the kitchen where my wife, Judith, was preparing dinner. It was time to ask.

"Jude, can you ask your therapist if I can see her?"

She stopped chopping jalapeños and looked up abruptly, her gold and chocolate curls bouncing away from her face. She adjusted her pink glasses and shifted her weight off her sore knee.

"Really? Okay, babe," she said gently.

Naturally, she was surprised. I had previously and repeatedly proclaimed that therapy was not for me and that I had control over my own thoughts, behaviors, and life. She had patiently accepted my claims and assumed I would never change.

Judith's therapist appropriately referred me to another therapist, Alessa Dolcetti.

. . .

A few brown leaves swirled on my windshield. I sat behind the wheel, tense from temporalis to peroneus. I was anxious about calling for an appointment with Dr. Dolcetti. My experiences with therapists were limited. Plus I knew next to nothing about her. I dialed anyway.

"You have reached the confidential voice mail of Dr. Alessa Dolcetti. Please leave a message, and I will return your call as soon as I can. Thanks."

BEEP.

Using my lowered, professional tone of voice, I left a message.

"Yes, hello, my name is Frances Southwick. You were recommended to me by another therapist, and I'm calling to set up a new patient visit. My number is . . ."

The following day at work, my phone buzzed in my right pocket as I walked out of a patient room. My breath stopped and my heart leapt. I scurried to the back of the clinic and hunkered by the children's bookshelf, out of sight and earshot of patients and staff. I looked at my phone.

A local number. Maybe it's Dolcetti.

I held the green button and swiped to answer.

"Hello, this is Frances," I said, trying to sound like a doctor.

"Hello, Frances. This is Alessa Dolcetti. I believe you left a message for me. Is now a good time to talk?"

"Yes, I have a few minutes."

"Great. How can I help you?"

Anxiety surfaced, but I felt hopeful and excited, too.

"Okay, thank you for calling me back so promptly. I'm a fairly new physician, and I'm having some difficulty and stress acclimating to my work."

It seemed like a good story—better than anything else I could figure. I could not tell her I was daydreaming daily about various methods of suicide without knowing why. The visions often clouded my drive home from work, so I thought it might be job stress.

"Okay, that sounds like what I do, like it's something I can help you with. Would you like to set up an appointment?"

"Yes, that sounds great," I answered, a tentative smile on my face.

. . .

Dr. Dolcetti was a petite feminist with silver hair and a PhD in psychology. At my first visit I admitted that my past therapy experiences all came in pairs. First sessions involved easy get-to-know-you talk; second sessions prodded old demons, and I never returned for thirds.

She asked about my family, which surprised me. I thought we would talk about patients and job stress.

"Who was living in your home throughout your childhood?" she asked, sitting a few feet across the room from me.

"Well, it was my brother, James, and our parents, Gary and Delilah. My dad is a CEO type, and my mom is like my little sister. You mi—"

She put her pen down and looked up, eyebrows raised.

"What was that?" she asked.

What was what?

"Did you say your mom is like your *little* sister?" she asked.

"Yes! My little mom," I confirmed, smiling.

I explained how I felt that we were like best friends, and always had been, and how we had a great relationship. Dr. Dolcetti gave me a quick side glance and picked up her pen. I started again.

"You might notice me talking about Gary and Delilah individually; they are married and live together, but my relationships with them are separate."

We ended the visit at fifty-four minutes.

Our second session was similar but with more detail. The last few minutes wound toward Drake, one of the boys who lived in my neighborhood. I began to distance myself from Dr. Dolcetti, as I had with other therapists.

"Same time next Monday?" she asked, wagging her pen a bit.

"Um . . . why don't I call you to reschedule?" I asked, my eyes on the door.

I fidgeted, and my voice was a little shrill. Dr. Dolcetti did not move.

"Frances, you are going to have the instinct to not return here. Whatever happens, just get your butt back on this couch."

So I returned for a third session, even though my gut railed against it.

"How did your parents relate to Drake?" Dr. Dolcetti asked.

I tensed.

IN THE BEGINNING

To study psychological trauma is to come face to face both with human
vulnerability in the natural world and with the capacity for evil in
human nature. To study psychological trauma means bearing witness to
horrible events. When the events are natural disasters or "acts of God,"
those who bear witness sympathize readily with the victim. But when
the traumatic events are of human design, those who bear witness are
caught in the conflict between victim and perpetrator.
It is morally impossible to remain neutral in this conflict.
The bystander is forced to take sides.

—Judith Herman, *Trauma and Recovery*

My rural Colorado block was flat and quiet. Dandelions pushed
through the street's cracking asphalt. Two tattered "road closed" barri-
cades with red and white stripes deterred any potential traffic.

Four houses of brick and wood sat in a 2 × 2 arrangement, facing each other amidst the tumbleweeds. The houses had been part of a
planned development, but a logistical splinter ended the project after
only four houses were built. From ages zero to ten, I lived in the north-
east house on that tiny block with my older brother, James, and my parents, Gary and Delilah.

An adjacent field stretched for miles. It was perfect for exploring, filled with goat's head weeds and yucca. Just a few dozen yards down grew a patch of about ten brambly trees. The four of us kids who lived on the block called it a forest. I daydreamed of running away to the forest, of making a fort and living on my own.

The occupants of my house were paired: two parents, two children, two dogs, and two cats. The living room walls were covered with antlers and animal heads. We had bear rugs, a wolf rug, and a bobcat rug. Our home held so much taxidermy from Gary's hunting trips that friends who visited made comments repeatedly, and some declined later invitations to visit.

Gary and Delilah made sure we had sufficient education, food, clothing, entertainment, and activities. At home, I remember James playing with Micro Machines and He-Man figurines, playing video games, and working toward his black belt in tae kwon do. I played jump rope, took gymnastics lessons, and had slumber parties with my friends.

Delilah was an opera singer and the secretary of my elementary school. Her parents were in their forties when she was born; she said they were more like grandparents than parents. She had a brother and a sister, both significantly older than her, which translated to her only child-like upbringing. She said her dad was her best friend growing up; he was charming and funny and played with the neighborhood kids. He passed away years before I was born. She had a less close relationship with her mom, a devout Christian Scientist who passed away after refusing medical treatment.

Delilah weighed 117 pounds. Her body was noisy like mine. It cracked all over, from neck to sternum to toes. She burped loudly whenever she felt sick, and she cleared her throat frequently. What she liked most was to be alone at her sewing machine or piano. She was well-read, especially in biographies and historical and religious texts. She used a sort of accent and personality with most people, with a full and bright smile, an eagerly nodding head, and perfect enunciation, like a character in a stage play. She told me she did not like feeling forced to be a character in a play. It was exhausting work.

When it was only me and Delilah, I was delighted. We stayed up late watching TV on floor quilt pallets with trays of fruit, veggies, cheese, and crackers. We read books, organized closets, cleaned house, or nerded out on my homework together. I sat and listened to her sing and play the piano. We drove the half hour to the nearest suburban area to walk around the mall and goof off.

When it was just me and Delilah, I felt free. I loved her intensely.

Gary was an ex-athlete of many sports, namely football, basketball, and baseball. He had been more naturally talented at each of these sports than his only sibling, a younger brother. Gary's father had coached the boys' sports teams, and Gary later accepted a full-ride baseball scholarship to a university, where he served as the president of his fraternity.

Gary was proud of the phrase the yearbook staff printed with his high school photo one year: "It's better you don't know what he's thinking." He had a Philip Seymour Hoffman head, a Donald Trump swagger and smirk, large glasses, and a locking leather briefcase. He paradoxically believed that women should be educated, independent, and have the same opportunities as men, while at the same time ending arguments in our house (including those with Delilah) by saying, "I'm bigger."

Every season, James or I polished his collection of cowboy boots, which doubled as work shoes. Though Gary made his living as a banker, he thought of himself as an outdoorsman or cowboy. His favorite activities were hunting, fishing, and riding his horses. I was named after his beloved aunt Frances, who bought him his first rifle.

My time with Gary (or James and Gary) involved playing ball sports, golfing, going to sporting goods stores, tying flies, fly-fishing, attending gun shows, shooting BB guns, skeet shooting, making trips to the hardware store, reloading rifle shells, and hunting. Sometimes we butchered our elk, deer, or antelope meat and then packaged it for the freezer. Gary and James would boil and mount the antlers.

To put it politely, these were not my interests, and honestly these activities were hard for me to get through, but when forced to participate, I tried to be "one of the guys." I fished. I shot guns. I killed animals. I occasionally felt proud to be an accepted part of the male team, but overall, these were not happy moments for me, not at the time, nor in retrospect.

Time together as a family included going on weekend skiing, hiking, and horseback riding trips (led by Gary), doing yardwork (also led by Gary), attending James' sporting events (some coached by Gary, while Delilah kept score and I played under the bleachers), and seeing movies (usually picked by Gary, e.g., *Comes a Horseman, Blade Runner, Silence of the Lambs, Tequila Sunrise, Unforgiven*).

. . .

Noah and Drake, boys my age, lived as only children with their parents in the two houses across the street. Gary was usually at the bank or away hunting, and Delilah was perpetually busy with work, music, and all the details of daily living (cleaning, cooking, ironing, gardening, changing lightbulbs, shopping, paying bills, and more). Noah's and Drake's parents worked as well. Naturally, we were all encouraged to play outside, or at one another's homes.

Drake, Noah, and I romped in the empty fields almost every day. We trapped garter snakes and wolf spiders, swearing they were rattlers and black widows. We chewed on the sweet ends of grass stalks on our walks to visit The Drainout, a small concrete washout pit. We crunched through four-foot-tall snow drifts and built snow forts, recruiting James for two-on-two snowball battles. It could not be girls against boys; I would have been a team of one.

"Wanna come over?" Drake or Noah would ask.

I would be standing in the kitchen of my house, the sun burning my eyes as I spoke with one boy or the other through our screen door. After checking with the authorities, my answer was usually, "Sure." Not only my loneliness and interest in the next round of mischief, but also three sets of busy parents would lead to an affirmative response.

"Drake and Noah want to play," I would tell Delilah.

"You and the boys always find fun," she would say with a shrug.

Boots on, puffy coat zipped up, I would clang through the door.

"Let's ride bikes!" Drake or Noah would shout.

I would wheel my purple Huffy from the garage, and off we would pedal.

What else might a typical group of young children do? We probably did it. Do somersaults? Yep. Play basketball with a hoop over a garage? Sure. Make messes? Of course. Raid our fridges for ingredients to make magic potions? Certainly. Nice, clean fun among kids, who were playing like kids.

As might be expected, Drake and Noah developed an unspoken competition for my attention. There were matches of wit, wrestling, and who could make the loudest fart noise. But there was no contest. I loved Noah.

> "Sexual behaviors in children are common, occurring in 42 to 73 percent of children by the time they reach 13 years of age. ... Sexual behavior problems are defined as developmentally inappropriate or intrusive sexual acts that typically involve coercion or distress. ... Sexual behavior problems typically involve other persons (but still may include solitary behaviors) and sexual contact. Developmentally inappropriate behavior can be defined as behavior that occurs at a greater frequency or at a much earlier age than would be developmentally or culturally expected, becomes a preoccupation for the child, or recurs

after adult intervention or corrective efforts. . . . When there is a disparity in age or development between children engaged in sexual behaviors, it is common for the older child to 'take charge' of the activity, directing the younger child in what to do and threatening him or her to comply and 'keep the secret.' . . . In a clinical sample of children six to 12 years of age with sexual behavior problems, the most common comorbid diagnoses were conduct disorder (76 percent), followed by attention-deficit/hyperactivity disorder (40 percent) and oppositional defiant disorder (27 percent)." —Nancy D. Kellogg, "Sexual Behaviors in Children: Evaluation and Management"

Noah was tiny, my size. In fact, we held sway as the shortest boy and girl in our class throughout elementary school. He was freckly, ornery, and kind, and he had a pet iguana.

Drake was tall and muscular with piercing blue eyes and straight, blond hair that collected in matted chunks along his face. He still hails as the messiest person I have ever met. His mouth was tiny, and he ate with his hands, which was an unfortunate combination. He spit when he talked. One day while we were playing cops and robbers, he asked me to wear his balaclava. It was so foul-smelling, I could hardly bear to keep it on my face, but I did not tear it off because he had seemed so comfortable in it. It smelled like rotten, regurgitated milk. The combination of the balaclava's dark color, grime, and smell, and the suffocation it afforded, matched the way I felt around Drake. But I kept wearing it that day. I did not want him to get disappointed or angry.

When Drake, Noah, and I were all together, we were kids acting like kids. We made sly jokes.

"Guys, I just heard something," Noah would say with a blank, anxious expression.

We would all stop in our tracks in the big grassy field.

"Come on, Noah," Drake would counter, rolling his eyes.

"No, seriously. Oh my God. Run! It's a bobcat!"

We all would dodge cacti and prairie dog holes, bounding wildly toward home. Noah would slow and stop halfway there, doubled over with laughter, until his whole face was red and he could not speak.

"I got you guys!"

He was the best prankster of the group.

The two boys would annoy each other occasionally. Drake's snotty face or sucked-on coat lapel would touch Noah during a game of tag and Noah would reel back.

"Ugh! God, Drake, you are so gross!"

Alas, Drake was usually the one knocking at my screen door.

"Wanna come out and play?" Drake asked one chilly morning, his nose smashed against the screen door, bowing it uncomfortably.

We were four or five years old.

My guts kinked up in response, with a wave of nausea.

"I'll ask my mom," I replied.

Whenever I asked to hang out with Drake, Delilah's usual 100% "yes" reaction felt more like 95% "yes" and 5% "that boy is disgusting, why do you want to go outside with him, is this a good idea?"

"All right. . . . Be home for dinner."

I returned to the now-wet screen door.

"Sure," I said.

"I'll race you!" he replied, squinting at me.

I ran out the door after him, clomping at my top speed over the pavement and sidewalk, into the field. He always outran me easily, and this day was no exception. He sped ahead of me, running to the other side of the field. When he reached the end he turned toward me,

Francie, who ran little more than half his speed. As I approached he put his hands out for me to give him ten. I obliged, raising my hands up to slap his, and he pulled them away as I swatted air.

"Missed me, missed me, now you gotta kiss me!" he taunted.

He came closer and [initiated unwanted contact]. I shuddered and backed away, wiping my face with my sleeve.

"Let's go play at your house," I suggested, hoping to change the play theme.

"Okay, but first I gotta show you something," he said.

I was curious and disgusted, my usual combination of feelings around Drake.

TRIGGER WARNING: Sexual Assault

He walked me two fields over, down into a sandy bunker I had never seen before. Litter was scattered around the bunker, mostly broken beer bottles. Drake dug through a section of dirt and pulled out two pornographic magazines—not Playboy, but something with [sexual imagery].

"We shouldn't be looking at these," I said with a quiet, shaky voice.

He pressed on, flipping through the pages slowly. My heart was pounding. He came close to me and [initiated unwanted sexual contact]. I was involuntarily aroused, which made me even sicker.

I don't want to do this.

Why am I feeling this way?

I'm sick.

I need to get home.

"There is a loneliness that can be rocked. Arms crossed, knees drawn up; holding, holding on, this motion, unlike a ship's, smooths and contains the rocker. It's an inside kind—wrapped tight like skin."

—Toni Morrison, *Beloved*

Later I opened the screen door to my house and gently closed it behind me instead of letting it clang. I took off my coat and boots and walked quietly to my bedroom. I walked around my bed and curled up on the carpet with my hands locked around my shins, out of sight from the doorway. I rocked myself by moving my torso forward and back.

If only Noah had been with us.

Things like this happened only when Noah was absent. Nonetheless, I had no desire to tell Noah or anyone else about events like these with Drake. I did not want to get in trouble, and I did not want to think about them.

I laid there for a couple of hours.

Eventually Delilah called for me anxiously.

"Francie? Francie?!"

I popped into the hallway, swearing I had just been playing in my room. She paused her homemaking tornado to give me an odd look, then shrugged.

"Time to set the table."

...

"How do you feel when you start to talk about Drake and the rape?" Dr. Dolcetti asks.

I answer quickly, while I am still fluid.

"It's like I get frozen, sort of. Like I can't move," I struggle to explain.

I cannot give an emotional description.[14]

"Mmmhmmm," Dr. Dolcetti says while nodding and scribbling fervently on her 8 × 11 legal pad.

As I am explaining myself, I can feel [the tactile memory of unwanted sexual contact] gnarl through my body.

My breathing pauses mid-inhalation. I blink slowly. My gaze becomes fixed, unfocused.

"It looks like you are going somewhere, Frances," Dr. Dolcetti says.

She can see I am starting to dissociate. I mentally agree, but I am unable to convey as much.

I pay close attention to the feelings in my body—the stiffening, the locking, like I am becoming a mannequin.

"I think it's time to get a cup of water," she says.

At her suggestion, my stiff muscles loosen slightly into sticky, slow motion. I rise and teeter to the hall and manage to pour myself a cup of cold water from the water cooler.

...

Journal entry. September 9, 2015.

I want to consider, own, and integrate my personal story. I want to stop running away from my experiences. Understand them. Accept them. I want to express myself completely. Not only my reaction, or my first thoughts about that reaction, but the whole composition of my experience of a moment.

---

14 "Alexithymia" means having no words for feelings (van der Kolk 2015). During treatment, and even now, I struggle to use emotional terms to describe my experiences. I can intellectualize about why I am in a certain state, or describe the related anatomy and physiology, but I still work hard to label my emotions.

The first step is to understand the events on a cognitive level. This I can handle; it's the emotional integration that's much harder for me.

To do the cognitive work right I must freeze-frame a moment, then watch it in slow motion. Next I examine it meticulously through repeated viewings. Rewind. Play. Rewind. Play. It's a tedious process.

Experience something.

Have a reaction.

Notice my reaction.

Explore my consciousness of noticing my reaction.

Form an initial informed opinion.

Consider what others will think.

Respond to these imaginary others.

Assert a conclusion. A sum of possible knowledge through rumination only.

Lately I'm focused on my episodes. I call them "episodes" because I don't know precisely what they are. They are periods wherein my awareness changes when it comes to the world and my perceptions. They last anywhere from minutes to days. Though the episodes are not always the same, each one involves some combination of the following symptoms: slowed speech, slowed thinking, slowed movement, tingling, numbness, weakness, dizziness, memory loss, decreased visual acuity, altered color perception and/or visual field size, and altered hearing. They often arrive during my sessions with Dr. Dolcetti. I ruminate during and afterward, picking them apart.

What are the triggers, or the prompting events?

How can I prevent them?

What the fuck are they?

Here's an example.

I'm sitting on the couch across from Dr. Dolcetti. She asks a question, and suddenly I feel flushed. My right cheek begins to tingle, and my right eyelid starts to sag. The breath I'm taking in through my nostrils feels like a breeze tickling my brain and the backs of my eyes, threatening to extinguish the candle of my thought.

I feel dizzy, I mentally type into a hovering thought bubble.

Somehow Dr. Dolcetti picks this up.

"So what do you think your dizziness tells us?" she asks calmly.

She crosses her tiny, fifty-something-year-old legs and leans in. I cannot tell whether she is genuinely interested, if she is trying to reengage me out of fear, or if she is just doing her job and faking interest. Funny, I thought I was good at reading people. I can't/don't answer her.

"We haven't talked about your trip home in February. How was it?" she asks, head cocked.

I squirm, struggling to hold onto my vision and consciousness. I squint to block out unnecessary distractions, but this seems to compound the feeling that I'm drifting. The couch dissolves until I am sitting on blackness. The distance between me and Dr. Dolcetti stretches and contracts. Four feet. One foot. A hundred yards. A thick bubble forms around me and mutes my entire awareness. The room is darker now. I see less, and the world is pixelated.[15]

This is my physical state and my description of my experience. These are the first two levels of processing a memory fragment. I need to get to level three before I collapse.

Okay, I'm here. This is you, Frances. You're still here, sitting on the couch across from Dr. Dolcetti, and you're having the feeling you've had many times before. Don't panic. You are a person in a situation, and you can figure this out.

---

15 "When trauma is severe, freezing or dissociation are normal. In these moments, compassion for ourselves for having suffered such extreme loss is the appropriate response" (Bareja 2021).

I remove myself another step further for better perspective.

But what is happening to me?

The entire right half of my body is burning, tingling, and getting weaker.

I separate my lips to describe how I'm feeling. I stammer.

"I'm . . . I . . . hm," and then I sigh.

"Hmm," I start again.[16]

I'm a normal person, and I'm having a natural response to something. Right?

I'm crystal. Hard. Frozen. Not my aware, snappy self. Something ignited this. There had to be a last dash of solute to set this supersaturated solution of me into crystal.

"Frances, can you identify what triggered this?" Dr. Dolcetti asks.

---

16 Bessel van der Kolk says the following about neuroimaging studies of people with trauma: "When people remember their trauma, their whole frontal lobe goes offline. So, the whole part of the brain that has to do with thinking, figuring things out and telling you what's right and wrong goes offline. The speech center of the brain goes offline. There's a big hole in the speech center; it's as if people are having a stroke in Broca's area" (2015).

THE HOUSE, PART 2

. . . Eventually I watched the darkness seep into my room through the cracks. I had no mop, no bucket, and no carpentry supplies, so I helplessly watched it leak onto the carpets and stain the legs of the furniture. It was losing patience . . .

HE'S BIGGER

The violation of principles often involves sexual humiliation . . .
even those who have successfully resisted understand
that under extreme duress anyone can be "broken."

—Judith Herman, *Trauma and Recovery*

Not only is there the element of surprise, the threat of death and the threat of injury, there is also the violation of the person that is synonymous with rape. This violation is physical, emotional and moral and associated with the closest human intimacy of sexual contact. The intention of the rapist is to profane this most private aspect of the person and render his victim utterly helpless. The character of the event is thus connected to the perpetrator's apparent need to terrorise, dominate and humiliate the victim. . . . Rape by its very nature is intentionally designed to produce psychological trauma. It is [a] form of organised social violence comparable only to the combat of war, being but the private expression of the same force. . . . Rape survivors experience . . . symptoms on a physical, behavioural and psychological level.

—Rape Crisis – Cape Town Trust, "*Rape Trauma Syndrome* (RTS)"

When I was in the fourth grade, my family moved into a larger house several miles away. For me, this meant no more Drake for almost four years.

That changed in junior high school.

The junior high I attended was for seventh and eighth graders. The school building consisted of one hallway lined with mustard-colored lockers, half-sized and double-decked. The classrooms were paired on each end of the hallway, English and history on the far side, science and math on the other, around the corner from the gym. The building was a short walk from the four houses of the block I lived on previously and a skip away from the elementary school.

Although Drake was a bit older than me, he was in the class behind me. When I was in grade eight, he was in seven. We were forced to interact somewhat regularly; we passed each other in the yellow hallway up to ten times per school day.

I turned thirteen the September of eighth grade. I was still the smallest person in my class. I was still handed crayons at restaurants whenever I went out to eat with my family. My period would not start for another two years.

Drake was lanky and muscular and played center for the basketball team. His voice was in the awkward stage of changing.

TRIGGER WARNING: Sexual Assault

In October he stopped me at my locker.

"Hey Francie. We haven't really been close since you moved. Do you want to come over after school, and we can talk?"

I tensed up and quickly refused.

He asked me again the next day, and again I refused.

Then he asked me the day after that. And the day after that. And after that.

After a collection of denials, he tried another approach.

"We could play poker. Do you know how to play? We could play strip poker," he teased.

He showed me a deck of cards he kept in his locker.

I refused.

It was the same thing every day that week.

And every day for the next several weeks.

Eventually the idea did not sound so terrible. It seemed off, certainly. Something was not quite right about it. But I could not find something explicitly wrong. After all, we had been alone together so many times before.

"What do you say? Cards?" he asked with a smile.

"Sure," I said.

Oh, what could be the harm, honestly? Plus I had never seen *him* naked—maybe the shoe would be on the other foot this time.

We walked to his house together. The disgust and curiosity I used to associate with Drake returned. We walked through his front door, then down the carpeted steps into his basement, toward his bedroom. When we reached the linen closet, he stopped me.

"You know what's funny?" he asked, looking at me, then back at the linen closet.

"What?" I asked uneasily.

"At the top of this closet is one of my dad's guns. If I wasn't such a nice guy, I could force you to do anything I want."

He looked into my eyes, narrowing his and glaring straight into me.

I froze. I stopped breathing.

He's faster than me. I can't outrun him.

My heart rate shot up.

He walked me down the rest of the short hallway, which now felt a mile long, to his bedroom.

He's bigger.

He closed the door behind us.

[Multiple sexual assaults occurred.]

I do not remember the end, but it did end. We were in his living room.

"OK, you want to go on a walk?" he asked casually.

Yes. Let's get outside. I can't breathe. I could run away.

"Sure, yeah," I replied.

We began walking around the field, like we had years before. I felt like I was in a trance.[17]

"So what did you like best?" he asked jovially.

"I don't know."

Should I make a run for it?

"Did you like it?" he asked.

I almost vomited.

"Yes," I lied.

He began skipping.

"But what was your favorite? What was your favorite part?!" he demanded.[18]

---

17 "It has been speculated that PTSD may be a consequence of triggering the unmyelinated vagus as a primitive defense system, often in inescapable contexts, when mobilization defensive strategies cannot be employed. In this state, a lower brainstem system, more frequently employed by reptiles, is regulating peripheral physiology. This system reduces oxygenated blood flow to the brain and leads to fainting and experiences of dissociation" (Porges 2011).

18 "Sex offenders demand that their victims find sexual fulfillment in submission" (Herman 1997).

[A portion of the sexual assault] was flashing in my eyes and skin. I was being smothered. I had to say something to quell him.

"The, um . . . the [portion of the sexual assault]."

He giggled loudly and picked up skipping.

"[Slur! Slur!!!]"

He yelled at me and threw his head back, laughing pitilessly.

We were approaching the field's closest point to the high school, where a basketball game was underway.

Plenty of people. Safe.

I decided it was time. A bolt of energy burst through my body. It was painful—it started in my chest and shot down into my hands and feet, springing me away from him. I ran as fast as I could toward the high school, straight across the rural highway. I did not look if any cars were coming. I could hear him laughing the whole way.

I reached the high school and stumbled to a walk, my feet barely touching the ground. I was floating. The world was airier, distant. I saw a friend in the distance. I do not remember who it was.

I approached her.

"I just had a . . . I had a weird encounter. With Drake," I said. "I feel violated."

"Violated?" she asked with an expression that was a cross between concerned and skeptical.

Panicked, I chuckled inappropriately. I was ashamed and immediately began to backtrack.

"Just kidding! I'm fine. It was only a game. I'm fine. I'm kidding you."

She went along with the lighter tone, laughing with me.

I do not remember attending the basketball game, but I did.

I do not remember going home, but I did.

I remember walking into the bathroom upstairs. I slowly removed my clothes, stiff and hunched, terrified and trembling. I wanted to keep my clothes on for my shower. Either that, or take my skin off with them. I stepped into the shower, blasted hot water, and scratched myself hard with my nails, leaving red trails all over my body, some of which started bleeding. I cowered and cried in the shower on my haunches for a long, long time.[19]

---

19 This is an example of humiliation devolving into shame. Humiliation involves the victim attributing an insult to the abuser (i.e., "He is bad"), whereas shame involves the victim internalizing the problem (i.e., "I am bad") (Brown 2012).

DRIFTING

What I remember is a picture floating around out there outside my
head. I mean, even if I don't think it, even if I die,
the picture of what I did, or knew, or saw is still out there.
Right in the place where it happened.

—Toni Morrison, *Beloved*

"Frances?" Dr. Dolcetti asks.

She sounds measured, but I can feel her anxiety.

Confusion, tingling, slowness, ptosis, vision changes . . .

*This must be a migraine. . . . Or maybe not. Maybe it's a dissocia-
tive episode.*

I have read plenty about dissociative episodes lately. Periods of
eerie changes in someone's experience of and response to reality, often
found in victims of trauma.

The odd sensations are distracting.

My upper lip feels full of collagen, Botox, and lidocaine. My vision
is tunneling.

*Interesting. My musing about dissociation was immediately followed by a
physical reaction. But I can't stop it.*

Yep, must be onto something. Probably psychosomatic. Conversion disorder. Or maybe factitious. Maybe you're making this happen.

"I think . . . I'm . . . it's . . . hmm. Dissociation."

I cannot see Dr. Dolcetti, but I feel her presence. She is trying to ride this experiential train with me. She is slanting further toward me.

"Okay, Frances. I see that you're going somewhere. Can you identify what triggered this?"

The intensity of her voice has climbed.

She's scared she won't be able to get me back by the end of the session. It'll make us go into the next client's time. I'm so stupid. I need to snap out of it. What's wrong with me? Why do I keep letting this happen?

...

TRIGGER WARNING: Sexual Assault

I smell the plasticky, sweaty, rolled-up wrestling mats.

Tennis shoes screech on the shiny court. Shouts echo from coaches and parents.

Drake and I are in the bleachers at a high school basketball game.

We are thirteen years old.

"Listen Francie, I've been feeling bad about what happened at my house. Why don't we make up?"

He looks sincere. His body language shows remorse; he is leaning in and his eyes are wide and sad.

In response, I uncross and recross my legs. I am unsure.

"We could go on a quick walk. What do you say?" he poses.

Hm. There is no way he has the gun here at school, which is reassuring.

"We can just walk down the hall, listen it's no big deal—let's just talk a minute," he says.

My chest feels a bit hollow. I want to help him.

"Okay," I agree.[20]

We walk as we have walked hundreds of times before.

After threading through the long hall of lockers connecting the high school and junior high, we reach a secluded part of the school, a sunken stairwell just outside the Home Economics room. We ease down into the nook and sit facing one another.

I smile and look into his eyes.

They are no longer wide and sad.

I stop breathing.

"On second thought, I think I liked what happened at my house. I want to do something like that again," he fires.

I am paralyzed.

He flexes his muscles and pulls a quarter from his pocket.

I try to speak and physically cannot. Like in a dream of mine, where a wolf is about to chase me in a field.

Slow motion.

Paralysis.

I cannot move.

He flips the coin in his fingers, over and over.

I cannot speak.

I can scarcely breathe.

[Sexual assault occurs.]

---

20 "The phenomenon of repeated victimization, indisputably real, calls for great care in interpretation . . . a well-learned dissociative coping style also leads survivors to ignore or minimize social cues that would ordinarily alert them to danger" (Herman 1997).

I run back down the hall we had walked before, but the hallway has stretched to several times its previous length. Running seems even slower than walking.

COPING

Many self-destructive behaviors can be understood as symbolic or
literal reenactments of the initial abuse. They serve the function
of regulating intolerable feeling states, in the absence of more
adaptive self-soothing strategies.

—Judith Herman, *Trauma and Recovery*

Musical Augmentation: "Going Down" by Ani DiFranco

Three weeks in, I was drowning in the intensity of the work of
therapy. My nightmares flared up, and my insomnia was worse than
ever.[21] My subconscious mind began belching up toxic, repressed material. I spent a few evenings crouched in a corner, bracing myself, shaking
and crying as I had many times before.

...

---

21 "Nightmares and insomnia are some of the most ubiquitous, distressing, and chronic
symptoms of Posttraumatic Stress Disorder" (Nappi, Drummond, and Hall 2012).

Journal entry. September 27, 2016.

To distract myself, I sit in chilled water, unmoving, my legs out-stretched, and my back curved into a lazy C shape, limp. I stare ahead toward the faucet. Jude is out at a gig. I'm alone. I'm empty. My thoughts are turning black again. I start to shiver.

I used to take three baths a day.

During a few months in college, I lived in a small house near the university campus with three hardly known, barely seen female roommates.

During the day I walked a mile and a half to campus to "wash dishes" in a research lab. This entailed collecting glass beakers, test tubes, flasks, and other gizmos from five stations in the sticky-floored biology lab. I arranged them according to size and breakability on large metal trays and loaded them into an odiferous autoclave. I felt like I was making the glassware suffer, subjecting it to extreme heat, steam, and a smell I still can't describe. The stench made me nervous. It felt danger-ous, like if I breathed more than once while loading or unloading the autoclave, I might develop a rare lung or brain illness. I felt prickly and itchy by the end of my shift. At the time, about half of the skin on my body was raw, dry, and bleeding in some places due to contact dermatitis from the lab, eczema, and my bathing ritual.

Back at the house, I would click the lock open with a key, or if I had forgotten the key, which was quite common, I would crawl through a dog door in the back of the house. Usually no one was home. The absence of humans made me feel uneasy. My jaw would tighten and my breathing would become faster and shallower. My upper arms would fix themselves to the sides of my torso. I would try to pee, which could take upward of two minutes of alternating attempts to relax or strain.[22]

To try to calm the distress, I would eat something.[23] Then I would eat too much of that something. Once it was bran muffin batter Delilah had made for me. She had come for a visit and left it in my fridge so I could pop it into a muffin tin and bake treats whenever I craved them. I never baked it; I ate the cold batter by the spoonful. It tasted tangy, metallic, and sort of like day-old oatmeal.

Whenever I had eaten too much, I would feel nauseated and panicky.

A bath, I would think. *A bath should help.*

I'd grab my towel from my bedroom and lock myself in the bathroom, turn on the tub faucet as hot as it would go, steaming the air. The mirror and thickly painted walls would sweat and dribble.

[Then I would perform a self-injurious activity.]

My attention would dull, my peripheral vision would gray out, and I would remain in a hazy daze for minutes to hours, alternating between vomiting and sitting in the scalding bath.[24]

---

22 Difficulty initiating urination is a chief complaint for some trauma survivors; they may present to a family physician, internist, urologist, or neurologist without realizing the connection between micturition and trauma. The psoas muscle is often contracted in times of post-traumatic reactivation, and it is intricately connected to the abdominal diaphragm and abuts the ureters. "Psoas contracture or spasm may also cause the fascias to adversely affect ureteral function" (Kuchera and Kuchera 1994).

23 When triggered, people with PTSD sometimes eat, an effort to activate the rest-and-digest portion of the parasympathetic nervous system, which can calm the intense activation.

24 Though the eating/bathing/purging/self-injuring ritual worsened my physical symptoms and shame, it was a sincere attempt at healing (van der Kolk 2015).

THE HOUSE, PART 3

We found that a history of CSA [child sexual abuse] is associated with increased risk of MDD [major depressive disorder] and suicidal thoughts and behavior including suicidal ideation, persistent suicidal thoughts, suicide plan, and suicide attempt (both lifetime and recurrent). These risks were somewhat reduced in magnitude, but largely remained significant, after controlling for MDD and PTSD. Survival analyses . . . confirmed that individuals with a history of CSA have increased risk for subsequently-occurring suicidal ideation and suicide attempt.

—Saaniya Bedi et al., *"Risk for Suicidal Thoughts and Behavior After Childhood Sexual Abuse in Women and Men"*

Eventually, often in the third or fourth decade of life, the defensive structure may begin to break down. . . . The façade can hold no longer, and the underlying fragmentation becomes manifest. When and if a breakdown occurs, it can take symptomatic forms that mimic virtually every category of psychiatric disorder. Survivors fear that they are going insane or that they will have to die.

—Judith Herman, *Trauma and Recovery*

. . .

It began to puddle on the floor, soaking the hems of the drapes. Then the drywall burst in all at once. The sludge rose forcefully, and I struggled to stay afloat. I turned my face sideways, then flipped to my back to keep my lips above the surface. I treaded and dog-paddled, searching for a window or door, but soon it rose to the ceiling and I was submerged. I held my breath as long as I could, until I tired and submitted. I let the black tarry oil rush into my nostrils and fill my mouth. I coughed and swallowed.

Now, only black . . .

WALLS COLLAPSE

Language, when finally it comes, has the vigor of a felon pardoned after twenty-one years on hold. Sudden, raw, stripped to its underwear.

—Toni Morrison, *Love*

TRIGGER WARNING: Suicidal Behavior

I came home from therapy in a daze on December 13, 2014. Dr. Dolcetti and I had been working together for about a month. I had started a prescription for citalopram for myself a few weeks earlier and notified my primary care doctor, who had tentatively agreed (over the phone, as I declined a same-day appointment) that I should be taking this medicine, and I was scheduled for a follow-up appointment.

I opened my laptop and typed without thinking. In the span of two hours, there was the story of Drake's assaults. It was written in awkward little sentences. Like a bad poem. I read it and then kept rereading it. I wrapped myself in a gray fuzzy blanket and waited for Jude to get home, trembling.

Flashbacks began to flicker in my mind's eye. [I experienced a tactile sexual assault memory, and then another.] It felt like it was really happening. [Then a tactile sexual abuse memory arose.]

I can't breathe.

Not a memory. Happening.

I started dry heaving. My hands squeezed the blanket tightly.

The key turned in the lock of the front door behind me, and the door squeaked open.

"Hi, babe . . ." Jude said carefully once she saw me on the couch.

She sat two seats away from me on the couch. My breathing quickened and shallowed.

"I can't do this!" I cried.

I felt fear-stricken, nauseated, dizzy, sexually aroused, ashamed, and desperate to make the thoughts, emotions, and sensations go away. They were overtaking me. I involuntarily curled into a ball while easing myself from the couch to the floor. Jude sat and watched helplessly. I motioned for her to look at the laptop. She read the disjointed story and began to cry, which ended my hysteria. I was suddenly hazed and numb.[25]

"I don't think I can go to your show," I said slowly, monotonously.

Jude was going to be directing the music for a teen play that evening. Yesterday had been the premier. Unbeknownst to her, while she had been setting up the stage and organizing the kids before the show, I had been sitting in our tub, contemplating [suicidal behavior]. The water was lukewarm when there was a knock on our front door, so I rose, dried off, and dressed myself to answer the door. It was her codirector. He needed the microphone stand Jude had left at home. It had been the closest I had ever come to ending my life.

Jude nodded.

---

25 This is an example of dissociation paired with projective identification (a neuropsychological coping strategy to create distance between the human and the emotion via verbal or nonverbal communication of the emotion to another human, and to observe the emotion in that other person).

"Okay, yeah. Are you okay? I mean are you going to be okay while I'm gone?" she asked pointedly.

"Mmmhmm," I replied, drifting. "Just drop me off at Salman's house."

Salman was a close friend and advisor who lived a few minutes away.

Jude agreed. She anxiously fixed her hair and makeup for the show. I gathered a blanket, hat, and scarf to cover myself as much as possible.

We pulled up to Salman's house. Jude walked with me up the steps. Though I knew Jude was in a hurry, my feet were clumsy and slow. One foot, then the other. One foot. The other.

Salman opened the front door. I stumbled inside and found my way to his couch. I hunkered there, waiting for him and Jude to say goodbye to each other. He closed the front door, walked to me, and sat beside me on the couch.

"What do you want to do?" he asked.

The question made me dry heave. It was a question Drake had repeated many times during his assaults. Salman automatically moved away from me slightly, then thought better of his reaction and leaned toward me again.

"Want to watch a movie?" he asked.

"Okay," I said in a wobbly voice.

He flipped through channels and found a Pixar film.

"Here we go," he said, trying to reassure us both.

He clicked play.

The torrent of emotion, memory, and physical response rushed forth again. Tears and mucus quickly formed streams down my face.

"I just . . . need some water," I said as I slowly stood and shuffled into the kitchen in search of respite.

I opened cupboards in slow motion, looking for a cup, but I was overwhelmed by the task and crumpled against a wall and down to the linoleum, shuddering and weeping. Salman appeared and handed me a cup of water. He looked at me, confused, concerned.

"I'm dealing with a lot. Therapy. I'm dealing with, um . . ."

I tried to get it out.

He was patient. I began rubbing my forehead over and over.

"It's . . . I'm working on . . . childhood . . . sexual abuse."

I finally got it out and began gasping and crying in loud bursts.

My filter was gone.

After a few minutes I asked, "Do you think—you think I should call my therapist?"

"I do," he replied.

He suggested that I make the call upstairs for privacy. I agreed. I followed him up three flights of steps at a sloth's pace. One foot. The other. One foot. The other.

We reached his bedroom and bathroom suite. I sat on the floor, and he gently closed the door, then walked back downstairs. I breathed progressively faster and higher in my chest.

I searched for "Dolcetti" on my cell phone and her number popped up. I dialed. After a few rings, I got her voice mail.

"You have reached the confidential voice mail of Dr. Alessa Dolcetti. If this is a psychiatric emergency, please call the Crisis Network at 1-800- . . ."

I let the recording trail on without listening.

BEEP.

"Hi Dr. Dolcetti, it's Frances. I'm . . . could you please call when you get this?"

I sat down on the rug with my legs outstretched. I rubbed my fore-head again. I could not put a full thought together. Partial thoughts came and went, interrupting one another.

I should call . . .

I wonder what would happen if Jude . . .

Jude is probably starting . . .

[A tactile sexual assault memory arose.] I started gagging.

I can't do this. I can't do it.

[Another tactile sexual assault memory came up.] My whole body pulsed violently.

[Now a sexual abuse memory.] I gagged again.

[Now another tactile sexual assault memory.]

[And another tactile sexual abuse memory.]

I can't do this.

I looked for a weapon. Something sharp or blunt, it did not matter what. I could not think straight to find something proper.

[I performed self-injury.]

The intensity of feelings and memories persisted.

I searched the bathroom for something but found nothing. I walked back to the bedroom.

I'm dizzy.

I can't do this.

I can't.

[I exhibited suicidal behavior.]

I had a vision of Salman finding me half-dead, then getting me to the hospital both too soon and too late, in a vegetative state.

Stop.

I shoved my hand in my pocket and fumbled for my phone. I dialed Salman's cell.

"Hello?" he asked, confused.

"Salman, can you come get me?"

He appeared seconds later. He was breathing fast and hard, and his energy was frantic. He hugged me close. We sat on the rug outside the closet. I was exhausted. I did not care what I looked like. I might as well have been naked. Salman phoned Jude.

"Jude? It's Salman. Yeah. . . . Yeah. I'm very concerned about Frances. Yes. We are going to go to the hospital. Yeah. We'll meet you there."

I was in the fetal position in the passenger seat of Salman's SUV when Dr. Dolcetti called. Salman eased us through Squirrel Hill and headed toward the psychiatric hospital. It was dark. There was little traffic.

"Hello?"

"Yes, Frances, it's Dr. Dolcetti. You called?" she asked calmly.

I was in a daze again.

"Yeah. I, um . . ."

I described [my suicidal behavior].

"I'm on my way to the DEC."[26]

"Oh. Oh, no. Oh, no. I . . . I will meet you there," she responded quickly.

I was relieved to be in Salman's car. Relieved to be going somewhere.

Lock me up. Lock me up away from myself.

Salman was composed during the drive, or he appeared to be. He pulled into a spot in a parking garage. I unbuckled my seatbelt, cracked

---

26 The Diagnostic Evaluation Center (DEC) is the psychiatric emergency department at the University of Pittsburgh Medical Center.

the door open, and slowly straightened my legs out enough to walk. Once I was upright, I started gagging again.

I plodded behind Salman, down a hill, into the lobby of the DEC. We were greeted first by security. They had me sign a clipboard. I slowly wrote my name and dated it.

"12/13/14."

Twelve, thirteen, fourteen.

MINDFULNESS

In both Buddhist meditation and Western somatic-based therapy, the process of experiencing and accepting the changing stream of sensations is the alchemical grounds of transformation.

—Tara Brach, "The Healing Journey: Rosalie's Story"

Musical Interlude: "Studying Stones" by Ani DiFranco

Prose. January 26, 2015.

"So, Frances, what did you notice?" Susanna asks in her abrasive, measured tone.

I squint at her freckled face to blur the scorch of her direct eye contact. The other women in the group squirm in the uncomfortable blue chairs. We sit in a horseshoe shape with Susanna slightly removed, topping the U.

"Um," I begin.

I sift through the previous sixty seconds for a bit of intelligible fodder.

"I was mostly able to focus on my breathing," I say.

"Did you drift?" she asks, as she always does.

"A little," I mumble.

I already know her next question.

"To the past? Future? Worries? Judgments?"

I've been in intensive group therapy for four weeks now, since leaving the hospital. There are nine of us women learning skills to cope with our lives.

Opposite action.

DEAR MAN.

Nonjudgmental stance.

Mindfulness.

In every three-hour session, our red-headed, giant-smiled, impenetrable group leader guides us through a minute-long mindfulness exercise. Last week she handed out pieces of sweet mint gum and asked us to be fully mindful of the experience of chewing it for one minute. Then she methodically asked each of us the same roster of questions.

This week she told us to focus on our breath. We were asked to observe our breath while staying present. Any thoughts and feelings that came up were to be acknowledged and allowed to float by.

I was bombarded by thoughts and feelings during the exercise. It was like flipping through channels on a wall of televisions.

Shame. A flash of Jude crying at the dining room table. Peace. The taste of a piping hot peppermint latte. My work shoes skidding on ice outside the therapy office as I rush to make the first minutes of group. Nausea. [A sexual assault experience.] Paralyzing terror. The cold tile of the shower on my back. Suffocation. Love. The reflection of a window in the glass of a painting Jude gave me for my birthday last year. My mind returns briefly to the room. Angelina, one of the other women, is shifting in her chair and suppressing a cough. Pain. My shoulder aches from carrying my laptop. Hunger. Should I make that frozen pizza for dinner, or save it for a more exhausting day?

"Past," I reply.

"And were you able to come back to a mindful space?" she asks.

No.

"Yes, I was," I lie.

"Great. OK, Charmaine, what did you notice?"

Once the pressure is off me, I disappear again, my mind wandering.

I see the image of me hunkered down on the leather passenger seat of Salman's SUV, embodying the same paralyzing fear and helplessness I felt almost twenty years prior in Drake's basement. We are driving through Squirrel Hill to the hospital. I'm starting to get slower, to daze, to float away.

Susanna would tell me to ground myself.

"Feel the chair holding you up. Feel your feet on the ground. Get immersed in the physical experience of the moment," she would say.

I feel the plastic chair under my corduroy pants. I look down at my shoes. Brown leather with creases at the base of the toes and splotches from the wet sidewalk.

The world around me begins to seep back into my consciousness.

Purple linoleum. The clearing of throats. Footsteps in the hall.

I watch as Susanna and Charmaine talk about the exercise. Charmaine's head is down. She tucks a lock of greasy brown hair behind her ear.

I am in and out for the remainder of the session. My attention waxes and wanes like a camera lens focusing and blurring. Like the sound of a landline dial tone flexing and releasing as I hold my ear to the receiver. I retreat into my mind, then into the room. Back to my mind, then back to the room.

I begin to detect a pattern. I don't fight it. I observe its peaks and valleys, detaching from expectation and judgment. I simply notice what is happening.

I see myself tense at Drake's gun threat. But that's it—I *see* it. I don't feel it. I am watching from above, the boy intimidating the girl. I see the girl shrink and freeze. I see [the sexual assault]. I watch him humiliate her. She finally runs away.

I feel nothing. I fade back into the room.

"OK, Frances," Susanna says.

I glance at the schoolroom-like clock. Five minutes left.

I feel less panic-stricken. My shoulders have relaxed a little, and I have another inch of distance from these relentless thoughts. I can't believe it helped.

"What skill do you want to work on?" she asks, leaning in with a gentle smile, tilting her pen back and forth between her fingers.

A beat of silence.

"Mindfulness."[27]

---

27 "Mindfulness is always at the core of just about any program I know that works for trauma" (van der Kolk 2015).

THE CUTE LITTLE GIRL

Not tall or ugly or bullying or mean,

Not menacing or competitive or disgusting.

She is cute and take-able.

Like a doll or an end-table.

Like a gleaming pebble.

You don't know why, but you put it in your pocket.

She wants to make you happy.

It feels so good,

It is so natural.

She is your personal delight.

She loves you, too.

Lolita could be any age.

She is enjoying every moment—no harm done.

Twenty-five years later,

The pebble grows a brain, eyes.

It is sitting in a pocket at Goodwill

It suddenly remembers being taken

Stranded now, it must actually grow extremities

And crawl out, jump to its possible death

Then walk, hopefully unnoticed

To the street

Where it can begin a life

Is it the first of its kind?[28]

---

28 I wrote this poem to express transcendence of helplessness and depersonalization. Please also read Mary Oliver's poem "Looking for Snakes" in her 1990 compilation, *House of Light.*

GARY

Psychological trauma is an affliction of the powerless. At the moment
of trauma, the victim is rendered helpless by overwhelming force.
When the force is that of nature, we speak of disasters. When the force
is that of other human beings, we speak of atrocities.
Traumatic events overwhelm the ordinary systems of care
that give people a sense of control, connection, and meaning.

—Judith Herman, *Trauma and Recovery*

Gary and Delilah's relationship began in high school when Delilah
was a sophomore. She had a crush on Gary, a senior. They went to a
school dance on a date, which led to a tumultuous on-again, off-again
relationship of seven years before they decided to marry. Delilah's parents did not approve of the relationship, while Gary's parents were
happy to have a young woman in the family.

The proposal involved a phone conversation about how Delilah's
lease was up, during which Gary suggested that Delilah move in with
him. She accepted the offer. They moved hundreds of miles away from
the town they had both grown up in with plans to build Gary's bud-
ding business, where he worked as a hunting and fishing guide. After
that heartful but doomed venture (his partner had allegedly abandoned

the business and ran away with the little profit they had earned), Gary changed paths and began working at a bank in a nearby small town.

Delilah did not want kids, but she eventually acquiesced to Gary's desire and was pregnant with James a few years after their move. A few more years after that, I was born.

Year by year, Gary worked his way up the rural banking ladder by capitalizing on his undergraduate degree in business, his leadership prowess, and his privilege. He was eventually promoted to the CEO position of several rural banks.

When I was about ten years old, the bank repossessed the biggest house in town, known in the area as "the house on the hill." It was literally the only house on the only hill as far as the eye could see. Gary bought the house for a bargain, and it became our new home.

One evening, after living there a couple of years, Gary, Delilah, and I were in the master bathroom. I was watching them get ready for an outing, buttoning their shirts in front of the wall-length mirror. I sat behind them on the bathtub ledge.

"How would you feel about driving a Jaguar?" Gary asked Delilah without looking at her.

Delilah stopped mid-earring-clasp, and her torso tensed. She let out a loud huff without looking at him.

"Gary, I told you, I don't want anything like that. The SUV is perfect—*more* than enough."

Gary kept getting ready at a steady pace, now placing cufflinks.

"I thought you'd look pretty good in a Jag," he smirked.

"Well, I've told you, I don't want one."

This was old information. Delilah hated diamonds and other pricey gifts. She was a coupon-clipper at heart.

"It's already leased. Three years. It'll be here next week," he replied evenly.

Delilah closed her eyes, clenched her jaw, and parted her lips to show her teeth slightly. Her reaction amused him. His smirk widened. My heart and neck tightened.

"Do I need to be here when it's delivered?" she asked.

"No, they'll drop it off. We'll leave the gate open.29 If you had to pick green or maroon, what color would you pick?"

Delilah rubbed between her eyebrows with her middle and ring fingers, eyes again closed.

"Green, I guess," she replied in a low voice.

"I got you the maroon one," he replied calmly.

Musical Augmentation: "Can't Buy Me Love" by the Beatles

---

29 An electric, remote-controlled gate had been installed the year prior, to stop break-ins from happening. Gary was the president of the only bank in town; this led to tension with some folks in the area, the result being periodic break-ins at our house.

EXIT

When fear rules, obedience is the only survival choice.

—Toni Morrison, *God Help the Child*

TRIGGER WARNING: Animal Abuse

"[*Intimidating phrase?!*]" Gary booms.

He kneels and snatches up the chewed garden hose. He looks at it, then slowly rises like a tidal wave and pivots toward the dogs, both already cowering. They know that voice, that look.

Gary keeps hold of the ragged end of the hose. The hose drags along the cement patio as he creeps toward the dogs. It unrolls from the spigot attachment.

Spottie, the dalmatian, has her tail between her legs. She shakes and winces. Her urine dribbles onto the concrete patio.

Gary spots the puddle forming. He leans back and laughs lusciously.

Sweet Girl, the golden Labrador, closes her eyes tightly and turns her head enough to show complete submission. She holds still, straining her ears to track Gary's figure as he approaches.

His laughing stops.

"[*Intimidating phrase?!*]" Gary repeats, glaring at Sweet Girl.

She lowers her head, and I hear her back claws scrape the cement as she braces her body.

I am a few feet behind Gary, holding a basketball, my body stiff. The sun is out. No wind. My eyes find Delilah.

She is inside, watching the scene through the sliding glass door. Her hair is pulled back, and she wears a strapless striped bikini top and wildly colored shorts decorated with random cartoon fruits, her clothes for lawn mowing. She hovers in the living room.

I can see her mental wheels turning.

Should I come outside? Or wait it out in the house? Should I interrupt his rage? Did he hit her yet?

She looks to me for a clue. Our eyes meet and conspire. Wordlessly, we decide to stay still.

. . .

After dinner Delilah and I sit cross-legged on the soft carpet of the living room floor. A new Scrabble board is between us. It sits atop a small turntable. We spin it and giggle like girls at a slumber party. The giggling is cut short by a bellow from the basement.

"Lilah? Delilah?!"

Her eyes flutter shut. Her jaw is tensed. We know she has to go. She sniffs in a noisy breath, hoists herself up, and stalks toward the steps, then down to the basement. I sit staring at my letters.

X, E, A, A, I, O, T.

She is gone for several minutes. Then several more. I get up and use the bathroom, then return to my Scrabble station to wait.

Eventually I hear her slowly ascend the steps. Too slowly. She usu-ally runs up and down the steps, her crackly joints a friendly alert she is nearby. She appears at the landing, her eyes red and swollen, her body trembling. She walks over and sits across from me again. She picks up two letters and starts to blubber. We sit for a while. I hold my breath for minutes.

"Are you going to tell me what happened?" I ask, my heart pounding.

In the past she has told me to be ready to leave at any time. Crying under the stairs at a ski lodge. Crying in the kitchen. Crying in the bath.

I am ready, I just have to grab my bag and the cats.

"He [physically assaulted] me. I swore I would leave if any man hurt me," she says, and this intensifies her crying.

I start to feel some excitement. Maybe it is really going to happen this time. I sit and wait for her directive. The tension grows a bit as we sit silently. I play my next word.

"E-X-I-T."

She looks up at me with an unsure glance.

. . .

Delilah is driving me to my piano lesson. She holds the steering wheel of the SUV carefully. It is a long, flat road from our small town to the city. I look out my window. Hay and dirt fields rush past my vision, giving me a head rush.

I feel heart-racy, as I often do. I slip off my purple sneakers and pull my knees into my chest to hug them, along with the soft beige seatbelt.

"What piece are you working on for the recital?" Delilah asks me brightly.

I can tell she is distracted by other thoughts, but I play along.

" 'Traumerei,' " I reply. "I love that piece so much."

"I know you do. I do, too."

She begins the old story.

"You remember that when you were a baby . . ."

"Yes, what happened?" I ask, my right cheek dimple showing.

"Well, you would sit in your highchair and listen while I played the piano. And one day I played 'Traumerei.' You whimpered behind me, so I stopped, and you stopped, too. I went back to the piano and picked up where I left off, and you started crying again. It was amazing. You were just a baby, but that song made you cry."

"I know, I can't believe it," I say with a little pride and wonder.

"It happened every time," Delilah says.

I close my eyes and hear part of the gentle piece in my mind.

Da, daaaaa, dum. Da, da da da daaaaa, daaaa . . .

I decide to ask.

"Are we leaving him?"

Delilah's face changes a bit. It relaxes and flattens out. It sort of sinks.

"Are you ready for the recital? Have you been practicing?" she asks in monotone.

I sink, too.

"Yeah, I've been practicing."

I look through the driver's side of the windshield. I see condos, signifying we are close to the city.

"He's a good man," she says in her flat voice.[30]

Musical Augmentation: "Love Me Like You Hate Me" by Rainsford

---

30 In *Toward a New Psychology of Women,* Jean Baker Miller writes, "Within a framework of inequality the existence of conflict is denied and the means to engage openly in conflict are excluded" (1986). Delilah frequently flipped back to denial as a means of survival. Anecdotally, I have learned that phrases like "he's a good guy" and "she's a great gal" are spoken with the subtext "let's not analyze this person's behavior; I'm close with them, and even if we find that they are despicable, or that the relationship is toxic and dangerous, I have too much at stake to end my relationship with them."

DELILAH

If I've learned anything at all about this life
It's the things that scare you the most
That are always worth the time . . .

—Brooke Annibale, "Patience"

Journal entry. September 24, 2015.

Drake is no longer what I'm focusing on in therapy. The most intense flashbacks from those sexual assaults are reducing in intensity after months of reflection and work. Now I'm trying to make sense of other things. It's not only the rape I have to work through. Something else is there. I need to find it. I need to forge clear opinions of myself and my experiences, to cross the next bridge.

I feel drunk, the paralyzed type. I lean my torso back and aim my attention toward the thrift store painting of a woodsy scene. I can see most of the details, but it's dark and grainy.

Don't get distracted. Identify the trigger. God, how do I do this? Stop it. You're in control.

I clumsily scan back through our session.

What were we talking about? The past few months. The winter. February...

Oh.

Dr. Dolcetti had mentioned February, summoning a flash memory of my visit home this year. Delilah and I were in the living room after the ski trip. Gary and the rest of the family had gone to bed an hour earlier. The right side of my neck was hurting. Delilah had offered to help. . . . Then came the right-sided symptoms.

Dr. Dolcetti is nodding in the periphery, it seems.

"I think . . . I need to focus . . . more on . . . focus more . . . on . . ." I get out slowly.

My symptoms are triggered by emotional topics.

Must be dissociation.

But seizures and heart attacks can be triggered by emotions, too. . . . Maybe it's a migraine. Or some other strange neurological condition. Demyelination? Partial seizure?

It doesn't matter. I know the next step.

"Delilah."

WE NEVER TALK ABOUT IT

Although the emphasis of the interviews with the women was on their own experience of [sexual] abuse at the hands of their mothers, they commonly, throughout the study, described their mothers as:

1. Emotionally needy and unstable; and

2. Committing boundary violations.

—Beverly Ogilvie, *Mother-Daughter Incest*

TRIGGER WARNING: Mother-Daughter Sexual Boundary Crossing

Delilah and I hung out a lot after school. I think the big boundary crossings started around fourth grade. I often sat at the counter having a snack while she ironed, sewed, or organized bills. She would put away her task, walk near to me, put her lips to one of my ears, and start crooning her version of Frank Lebby Stanton's *Mighty Lak' a Rose*.

"Sweetest little fellooooooooooooooooooooooow . . ."

I would squirm in anxious delight.

"Anybody knoooooooooooooooooooooooooowsssssssssssssss . . ."

She would draw out the O's to buzz my ear. I would pull away in discomfort and then present my ear for more.

"Dooooooooon't knooooooooooow whhhhhhat to call himmmmmmmmmmmmmmmmm, but he's mighty like a roooooooo-wooooooohhhh-woooooooooooooooosssse."

By the end I usually had a wild mixture of physical and emotional sensations involving my ear, head, body, and genitals. I would wipe the condensation out of my ear and shudder, brimming with angst and stimulation.

One day I pointed between my legs and said, "It makes me feel my heartbeat here."

She had smiled, giggled, and walked back to the ironing.

. . .

TRIGGER WARNING: Intimate Partner Abuse Witnessed by Children and Mother-Daughter Sexual Abuse

Nickelodeon blazes before me. First *Doug*, then *Rugrats*. I lay on my belly, knees bent, feet fidgeting in the air. I look back and forth between the TV and my pre-algebra homework.

Delilah is clanging about in the kitchen, chopping loudly, opening and shutting cupboards, preparing dinner. James is probably driving home from baseball practice.

Sweet Girl and Spottie start barking—Gary's home. His diesel chug-chug-chugs closer, louder, then ceases. A few moments later he opens the door. I turn the TV to a news station.

James arrives half an hour later. He drops his sports gear in the laundry room and plops onto a chair near me. I get up and walk to the dining room. I set out forks, knives, napkins, and tall glasses of ice water.

The four of us eat cooked carrots with potatoes and roast antelope from last hunting season. We are polite, with perfect table manners. Gary seems tired, unsmiling. Delilah flits between her seat and the kitchen for steak sauce and salad dressing.

Gary is the first to retire to the basement after dinner. He flings out the footrest on the recliner portion of the couch. Delilah curls up on the opposite side of the couch. James sits in front of the fireplace. I am on the floor, as usual (my choice). I wait to see what Gary will pick for the after-dinner movie. He slides *Batman*, the Michael Keaton version, into the VCR.

Partway into the movie, when the Joker is taking over Gotham City, Delilah creeps closer to Gary.

"Gary, give me a kiss."

"Quit it," he warns.

"Come on, just one kiss," she whines playfully, bringing her face near his.

"Quit it, damnit! Somebody's gonna get hurt!"

My brother and I turn to watch. I hold my breath with my shoulders hunched protectively.

Delilah makes one more attempt.

Gary's eyes widen and darken. He flips his attention to her face. He [physically assaults her], and her eyes fill up. He [physically assaults her again], and then he lets go, grinning.

"I told you. It's gonna end in tears."

She shrinks into the other side of the couch. I pack up my notebooks and climb up the stairs to where the other TV is.

I flip Nickelodeon back on. It's Nick at Nite. Mary Tyler Moore is tidying up her apartment. Dick Van Dyke is on next. My stomach is a little upset, and my breathing is shallow. I set my books around me on the couch and bundle myself in, my knees pressed against my lips. I tuck my legs into my sweatshirt and pull my arms in, too, so I become a legless, lumpy torso with a head. Nice and cozy. I go back to my pre-algebra.

The Dick Van Dyke Show is almost over now. I hear footsteps coming up the basement stairs. The crackling joints reassure me it is Delilah. I turn and watch as she walks toward me in her mid-thigh-length silk nightgown. Her footsteps are heavy, her eyes weary.

"Hi, France!" she tries to be bright but fails.

"Hi, Mom," I say.

"Want to rub backs?" she asks hopefully.

Her eyelids are red and puffy.

"What happened?" I ask, instantly holding my breath at attention.

Her face transforms easily, and she breaks down in tears.

"Okay," I reply.

I am almost done with my homework, anyway.

She [initiates sexual abuse].

It is weird. I always think I should stop her, but I never do.

And we never talk about it.

I walk to my room for bed.

I get rid of the weird feelings with an orgasm, as I always do.

I always think I won't, but then I always do.

I shouldn't.

Before I fall asleep, I pray for forgiveness over and over in the dark.

DIAGNOSIS OF C-PTSD

Sexual behavior is the most common behavioral
indicator of child sexual abuse.[31]

—Association for the Treatment of Sexual Abusers,
"Children with Sexual Behavior Problems"

"Okay, class. Time to line up for lunch," Mrs. Lehrer directs.

I take my time as a train of fellow fifth graders forms, ambling with Emma to the back of the line.

"Daniel wants to go out with you!" Emma bursts out.

"Tell him yes," I say automatically.

Daniel was fair game. Noah had moved to Illinois the summer before, and I had just broken up with John. Mark. Brian. The other John. There was a long roster. Plus Daniel and BJ split up yesterday. Perfect.

"So what did he say?" I ask.

"He told Tom, and Tom told me. He wants to see if you want to go out with him," Emma explains.

---

31 One of the criteria for c-PTSD is alterations in affect regulation, including compulsive sexuality, which may be evidenced by inappropriate (excessive or promiscuous) attempts to achieve intimate contact (including but not limited to sexual or physical intimacy), or excessive reliance on peers or adults for safety and reassurance (Herman 1997).

The kids behind Emma push her a little.

"Go-wuh!"

We walk single file over rough purple-blue carpet that transitions to scratched-up pale cafeteria flooring. It is Friday, so we can pick between plain milk or chocolate. I take chocolate.

"Well, are you going to tell him, or is Tom? And when?!" I ask.

"I'll get him at recess," Emma says.

She seems to have a plan.

"Okay, tell me what he says."

We arrive at the next stage of the lunch line. One by one we each produce our plastic red lunch cards. I look down at the label on my card, printed by the screeching dot matrix in the front office.

"SOUTHWICK,FRANC."

My name is too long to fit on the card.

Delilah puts her hand out for my card. I hand it to her; she swipes it briskly and returns it to me. We exchange a familiar glance but do not say anything. She is the school secretary, nurse, and lunch card swiper.

"Hi, Misses South-Wick!" Emma sings.

"Hi, Emma," Delilah replies with a toothy convincing-for-every-one-but-not-for-me smile.

I am not embarrassed by her but wonder briefly if I should be.

A few moments later Emma and I are magnetically pulled to the table our friends have chosen. Emma cannot keep it quiet.

"Daniel and Francie!" she announces.

The other girls have a variety of reactions that do not penetrate my boy-crazy bubble.

After I throw away most of my lunch (pear cup, soggy green bean pieces, chunk of hard turkey . . . I ate the roll at least), I push on the gray bar of the exit door, using stiff arms and all my weight to open it. The sharp wind sweeps my hair into my eyes. I push my hair back, and the wind blows it straight back into my face. I forgot to bring a pony-tail holder.

I look for my comradettes on the playground. Last year we jumped rope in groups of three, blue and white plastic tubes smacking the concrete just before our tennis-shoes, the pattern sounding like heartbeats. We were too grown up for that this year. I walk to the spider bars, climb to the top, and join BJ.

We sit and watch the boys organize into two teams and play touch football. Daniel is one of the quarterbacks. I beam. Already I identify him as my boyfriend. After a few plays Emma approaches Daniel and whispers something to him with a cupped hand. He nods like it is something about shoelaces or the weather. I cover my face in excitement. BJ climbs down and sulks away to the tire swings.

What's her problem?

The bell rings.

We shuffle into the building and my classmates hurry to sit cross-legged on the floor for the opening story. Mrs. Lehrer gives a ticket to the first student to sit in the circle. I watch Timmy take the ticket and tuck it away. My mind snaps back to Daniel.

A few other kids trickle in, laughing and wiping wind snot from their upper lips. They crowd around me. I start feeling a little pitter-pattery.

Where is he?

Daniel appears with Tom and John. They are slapping each other's backs, happy and loud. He sits down. Three kids sit between him and me.

"Okay, class, open your books to where we left off," Mrs. Lehrer instructs.

Oh yeah, books, it dawns on all of us at once. We rise and scramble to our desks, collect our weathered copies of *The Westing Game,* and gather again. This time I wait for Daniel to sit with his friends first, then I quickly sit nearby. Now there is only one human obstacle between Daniel and me. Tom.

"Kara, why don't you start us off?" Mrs. Lehrer offers.

Kara opens her book.

"Mrs. Wexler gasped; it was breathtaking, all right . . ." she begins quietly.

I make my move. I tap on Tom's knee with my tennis shoe. He looks over at me. I motion for a switch. He understands instantly; we all know the code for switches. I pretend I am stretching and crawl forward behind Timmy. Tom scoots behind me to take my spot; I simultaneously push myself into position, next to Daniel. We are motionless again. I look at Mrs. Lehrer, who is reading along with Kara, suggesting that our movements were undetected.

Daniel does not look at me. I edge as close to him as I can. I look over at Emma and motion for her to get Kristen to cover. Emma taps Kristen's knee and urges with her eyes for Kristen to cover. Kristen is nervous in her eyes and hands, but she obliges, positioning herself squarely in front of Mrs. Lehrer's view of Daniel and me. The stage is set.

I slide my hand over and sidle it beside Daniel's, touching the sides of our pinkies. His hand is a little cold. To my delight he tucks his pinky and ring fingers over mine. Nothing could top this moment.

I slide my hand further under his. He keeps his hand steady.

Yes. It is working so far. He really likes me.

I slide my hand up his forearm as slowly as I can, then move it to his thigh. His thigh shakes a little. I [make unwanted sexual contact]. He reflexively blocks me, bringing his knee up, thus pushing my hand away.

Hmph.

I look over again. His hand is further away but still on the ground. I make one more attempt, placing my hand on his. He shies away and folds his hands in his lap.

The next day Emma tells me Daniel wants to break it off.

Oh. He doesn't like me.

Huh.

I wonder if Ethan would go out with me.

. . .

Journal entry. March 5, 2021.

I want to be alone.

I want to have no ovaries.[32]

I want to have no physical self.

I want to be done.

I don't want drugs.

I don't want hospitals.

I want to be done.

I don't want to fight anymore.

I want to be alone and without sensation.

. . .

---

32 This is in reference to unwanted sexual arousal. One of the most painful pieces of life after sexual trauma is the neurobiological association between unwanted stimuli and sexual arousal.

Journal entry. January 24, 2015.

Funeral songs:

"One Voice," The Wailin' Jennys

"Wise Up," Aimee Mann

"Outside In," Chris Smither

"Down to the River to Pray," traditional

Green burial, if possible.

If not possible, cremation.[33]

...

Journal entry. February 10, 2015.

How many times and in how many ways have I tried to deny what has happened?[34]

I have asked so many medical and neuropsychological professionals about what is normal and not normal. I have read every article and reviewed every related blog I could find. I have read multiple books. I have written extensively about my experiences and have run it all past many intelligent women, looking for what the truth is.

Elva was the therapist for my patients and worked in the same office. She had a rich knowledge of abuse. After finding a woman with a history of child abuse who had previously seen a couple of therapists but never broached the abuse, she had wondered aloud, "What are they talking about in therapy??"

---

33 This illustrates c-PTSD criteria, including alterations in affect regulation, such as chronic suicidal preoccupation, alterations in systems of meaning, and a sense of hopelessness and despair.

34 This illustrates a criterion for c-PTSD: alterations in consciousness, including amnesia or hypermnesia for traumatic events.

This made me more confident in her opinion.

"Elva, let me ask you something. I have a thirteen-year-old patient who still bathes with her mother in a standard American tub, and the other family members are not involved.[35] What do you recommend I do?"

I lasered into her facial response. She seemed disgusted and saddened.

"That is not normal," she began.

"Right."

"That would not happen in isolation. There is more going on," she said.

"Okay, thank you," I replied.

Elva was usually brief in her responses, preferring to focus on time with clients and completing her notes.

I also asked our nurses what they thought about a situation like this. They were unsettled and had no direct response.

Dr. Dolcetti was clear that this situation was not normal. When I tried to get around it by suggesting that some families bathe at the same time, she knew where I was headed and stopped me short.

"Those are families who bathe in large tubs without contact. I'm guessing you are talking about an American bathtub? And, Frances, this behavior would not occur in isolation."

I blushed.

I found conflicting information regarding normal medically recommended ages for families to stop bathing together. I searched everywhere for information about mothers and daughters trading massages.

I asked Jude to run it by her therapist.

---

35 Communal bathing is a cultural norm for some groups, but the dimensions of the tub are significantly larger than the standard American bathtub. Furthermore, the exclusion of other family members is a red flag.

"Oh, that is a severely enmeshed mother and daughter," the therapist said.

That night, I searched and fell into a rabbit hole of information about mother-daughter sexual abuse, a.k.a. MDSA.

WHAMMMMMM.

It all fit.

...

Journal entry. January 29, 2015.

I stayed home from work today. They had to cancel a full day's worth of patients. I woke up and felt like I was dying. Didn't know why.

My sessions with Dr. Dolcetti are so hard. I'm in a daze for about twelve hours afterward. I dissociate multiple times each session, and it's tough on me. I stayed in my pajamas all day. I had a compulsion to get on my laptop and look up sexual abuse stories, as I have been doing lately. Sometimes it makes me better, sometimes the opposite—and I sink slowly until fully submerged in darkness for a day or so.

"The final step in the psychological control of the victim is not completed until she has been forced to violate her own moral principles and to betray her basic human attachments. Psychologically, this is the most destructive of all coercive techniques, for the victim who has succumbed loathes herself." —Judith Herman, *Trauma and Recovery*

"The issue of self-blame is almost universal in chronic trauma—it's pervasive throughout psychiatric practice because so many people are traumatized from infant and childhood experiences. It's always about blaming yourself for what you did or did not do during your childhood. . . . Shame becomes a meaning-making system [and] an important defense

that helps you in the future." —Bessel van der Kolk and Bill O'Hanlon,
"How to Work with Shame When It's Connected to Trauma"

...

Journal entry. April 21, 2015.

Because I didn't fight, I feel like I am also a rapist of the worst type—I raped myself. The ultimate self-betrayal. Worse even than suicide—because one doesn't have to live with what one has done to oneself after suicide. Add the shame I brought to my family. Add revictimization. Add secrecy and shameful eating disorder, self-harm, and sexual problems. You get a self-loathing person who doesn't want to live—but suicide is too good for her, so she just suffers quietly, fantasizing about her own death.[36]

---

36 This is an example of a c-PTSD criterion: alterations in self-perception, including a sense of defilement.

WAS HE REAL?

Every now and then she looked around for tangible
evidence of his having ever been there. . . . She could find nothing,
for he had left nothing but his stunning absence.

—Toni Morrison, *Sula*

A few months before my hospitalization, I began googling Drake's name over and over again.[37]

I eventually found something bizarre Drake had written, probably in high school. It detailed a young woman being held captive in a dungeon by two men, abused, attempting to escape, and being attacked. It is no longer available online, but I copied it.

I called one of our elementary school teachers. She confirmed that her son (one of Drake's close friends) had chosen not to send his child to public school . . . because of what had happened to me.

"Now Francie Southwick . . . there's a girl who suffered," she shared, were his words.

When they were seven or eight years old Drake had bragged to him about what he had forced me to do.

---

37 This is an example of a c-PTSD criterion: alterations in perception of the perpetrator.

I asked my parents what their earliest impressions of Drake were.

"I never trusted that kid," said Gary.

"I was always scared of him," said Delilah.

Delilah congratulated herself and Gary for putting me in the grade ahead of Drake, separating us slightly at school.

I used social media to contact childhood friends who knew him. One friend confirmed that he had been aggressive in pursuing me and that this had made me uncomfortable.

I looked through old yearbooks. I cut his photos out and gave them to Dr. Dolcetti to prove he was real. His face chilled me. One photo was of him standing with one foot on a teammate, pointing in his face and laugh-screaming.

I found his phone number online and called it (after blocking my number) to hear his low voice, then hung up after he said hello twice.

I needed to know he was real.

SEEKING FAIRNESS

FIRST TIME REPORTING

The reader might wonder, *Why didn't she tell someone?*

Why didn't she reach out?

Someone could have helped.

What about her parents?

What about, say, a counselor?

...

Even without diagnostic criteria or clues suggesting prior trauma, the most obvious sign of trauma is the victim reporting the trauma to a friend, family member, or trusted authority.

...

TRIGGER WARNING: Mass Shooting

"Have you seen the news?" my friend Neil asked.

I shrugged. It was April 20, 1999. I was fifteen.

"What news?" I asked.

"Two kids are killing everybody at their school," Neil said.

He motioned down the hallway. I walked with him to the high school library, where a TV on a gray plastic cart had been rolled out of a closet and plugged in. Students and teachers were gathered in front of it, staring. It was not clear what was happening. News footage from a helicopter was playing. The footage showed a large building with a tiny crowd outside of it, red and blue police and ambulance lights flashing.

That evening I shuddered and curled up on my couch as I watched the terrible events at Columbine High School on the news. Twenty-one injured. Fifteen dead. An arsenal of weapons. Black trench coats. Homemade bombs.

That last one plucked a nerve.

Bombs.

My thoughts traveled back to the four houses.

Drake and his dad did odd little projects. They would build a wagon or find old clay pigeons and take them out to shoot them. They were boys together.

One of Drake's loves was pyrotechnics. He had shown me black and gray film canisters filled with gunpowder. He kept them hidden in his sock drawer.

He had confided in a mutual friend about his aspirations for his death: the sexual assault of a woman or multiple women, followed by the televised murder of a crowd of people in a town square, followed by his own suicide.

I walked to the school guidance counselor's tiny office the next morning. The door was open. I knocked tentatively.

"Um, hi, Mr. Rainer. Yeah, can I talk to you?"

Mr. Rainer looked up from his desk.

"Sure, come in, have a seat," he replied with his scratchy voice.

He cleared a stack of papers from the chair he reserved for students. I tiptoed in and sat dow. I folded my legs up on the seat and wrapped my arms around my left knee.

"Okay," I said.

He leaned over and closed the door.

"Okay," he echoed.

We sat in silence for a few moments as I adjusted and readjusted my legs, cleared my throat, ran my fingers through my long hair.

"Okay," I started again. "I am worried about the school and about Drake Erebus."

He was unmoved, his face revealing faux-concern.

"What do you mean?" he asked.

"He is dangerous," I said.

My heart rate began its rapid ramp-up.

"I grew up with him, so I know him, and I think if the Columbine thing were to happen here, it would be Drake."

Mr. Rainer looked at me quizzically. I continued.

"Yeah, he keeps gunpowder in his sock drawer. He knows how to build bombs."

Now I had his attention. He leaned in toward me.

"Have you talked to anyone else about this?" he asked.

"No, I didn't, I mean I didn't take him so seriously until this thing happened yesterday," I said.

I was not eloquent when I was rattled. I needed to get the point across more effectively.

He could seriously blow up the school.

"He could seriously blow up the school," I spurted, and I started trembling.

Mr. Rainer noticed, and he softened his tone.

"How do you know him so well?" he asked quietly.

Mr. Rainer would not have known about the four houses; he had only worked in our school for a couple of years.

"I grew up right across the street from him."

I was trembling more, and my voice was wobbling.

"Mmmhmm," he said.

I was fairly comfortable around Mr. Rainer, so I was prepared to answer all of his questions. Somehow he was clever enough to ask questions until information about my sexual relationship with Drake trickled out. He asked me to write about those experiences and bring the writings to his office.

I returned the next day with two college-ruled sheets of paper folded up in the pocket of my jeans. Again I knocked on his open door.

"Come in," he said kindly, ushering me to the student seat.

He closed the door. I offered him the papers with a shaky hand and gathered my body onto the seat of the chair, arms around my shins.

"Do you want to tell me about it, or do you want me to read this?" he asked.

"You can read it," I replied.

No way could I verbalize the details. I could scarcely write them down the night before, balled up in my bed. Mr. Rainer unfolded the papers and smoothed them out on his desk. He took his time reading the text. His mouth opened and hung like a hinge. When he was finished reading, he turned to me slowly.

"Frances, have you told anyone about this?" he asked.

"No," I replied.

Oh, God, what's coming now? What do I have to do now?

"Frances, this was . . . this is *rape*," he said.

By his enunciation and awkward bluntness, it seemed like this was his first time saying the word out loud. I suddenly felt numb and still. My jaw was open, ready to speak, but my mouth would not move.

"We need to bring your parents in," he said matter-of-factly.

"No . . . no. Please."

I was suddenly able to speak again.

"You can't call them. Please don't tell them!"

"We have to do this, Frances. This is serious," he replied.

"No, please! Please. They are going to blame me! Trust me, they are going to freak out and hate me!" I said frantically.

I felt dread and desperation in my gut.

"They won't blame you. This is serious. We have to involve them; there is no question about it. We'll have a meeting tomorrow after school," he directed.

"Mr. Rainer . . ." I pleaded.

"Francie, if you don't bring them tomorrow, I will," he said definitively.

He was not going to budge.

"Okay, I'll bring my mom," I said, negotiating.

I would start with her. I would break the news to her first, then figure Gary out later.

Mr. Rainer agreed.

. . .

"It is very tempting to take the side of the perpetrator. All the perpetrator asks is that the bystander do nothing. He appeals to the universal desire to see, hear, and speak no evil. The victim, on the contrary, asks the bystander to share the burden of pain.
The victim demands action, engagement, and remembering."
—Judith Herman, *Trauma and Recovery*

. . .

I told Delilah that there was a meeting planned with Mr. Rainer and that he wanted her to be there. She was flippant.

"Okay, sure, I'll meet you there after school," she agreed easily.

She probably figured this would be a meeting about scholarships or a school club. I had never been in serious trouble at school. I did not correct her ignorance.

She arrived at 3:30 p.m., fifteen minutes after the last bell. No other students were in the building. I was already waiting anxiously in my chair in Mr. Rainer's office. She walked into the cluttered room and took the chair he had squeezed into the tiny office.

"Okay, what are we meeting about?" she asked brightly, sitting upright with her legs perfectly crossed.

"Francie has something she wants to tell you," Mr. Rainer said, his eyes aimed at Delilah. My heart gave a big *thud*. I tried to get his attention with my eyes.

I have to do this? I thought you were going to tell her.

He kept his focus on Delilah.

"Yeah, okay," I started.

My jaw froze, half open. My whole body froze. I blinked slowly. My peripheral vision was getting fuzzier and darker. We sat there for a minute or so, me in a fog, unable to talk.

"You know that you're not speaking?!" Delilah sputtered, suddenly impatient.

"Yeah," I said. "Yeah. I, uh, this . . . is about . . . Drake."

They were both staring at my face. I was gazing at the brass handle of Mr. Rainer's top desk drawer. Was it moving? Was I moving?

"So, Drake. At his house. He had me do . . . things," I said.

My heart was fluttering, speeding and slowing. I felt I might pass out.

"Yes . . . okay . . ." Delilah said, annoyed.

She got angry when she was confused or waiting. Right now she was both.

"He threatened me with a gun. Top of the closet, in the basement," I said.

I was done. I lowered my head and hugged my legs. No more.

...

Delilah drove us home in tense air. She clutched the steering wheel with her hands at ten and two.

"Well, are you going to tell your dad, or am I going to?" she snarled.

Crap.

"You," I said.

I imagined relaying this information to Gary. I pictured his eruption, either punching my face or squealing out of our driveway and heading for Drake's house with a rifle.

We arrived at home. I sealed myself inside my room and waited.

There was a knock on my door a few hours later.

"Your dad wants to speak with you," Delilah reported.

I walked with her to their bedroom and bathroom suite and sat on the edge of the tub. I often sat there talking with Delilah as she dressed or undressed. Gary stalked in, heavy with fury.

"Well, do you want to press charges?" he demanded, his arms folded.

This was unexpected.

What? What does he know about what happened? Which thing?

"Uh, I . . . don't know," I replied.

He snapped his body away from me with a snort. As he stormed out of the house, he said loudly, "I'm leaving. She doesn't care about herself, anyway."[38]

WHAMMMMMM.

He left for the weekend on an unplanned fishing trip.

---

38 In *Building a Life Worth Living*, Marsha Linehan writes: "Traumatic invalidation may occur only once, as when a mother refuses to believe her daughter is telling the truth when she reports sexual abuse, or when a witness falsely testifies that a person committed a crime he did not commit. It can be an accumulation of pervasive misreading of emotions by others, such as when someone insists incorrectly that a person is angry, jealous, afraid, or lying or insists that the person has internal motives he or she doesn't have. Trauma is most likely when these actions make the individual feel like an outsider. In the extreme, traumatic invalidation can lead an individual to thoughts of suicide and actual self-harm as a source of relief from the toxic environment they are in" (2020).

REPORTING TO THE AUTHORITIES

In the matter of criminal reporting, as in all other matters,
the choice must rest with the survivor. A decision to report
ideally opens the door to social restitution.

—Judith Herman, *Trauma and Recovery*

The reader might reflect, *Okay, they didn't exactly handle it well, but times have changed.*

She should at least report it now, make a police report.

...

After about eighteen months of therapy I decided to complete the circle. I mailed letters to Delilah and Gary, explaining that although they helped me tremendously, they had also hurt me significantly.

Soon after, I discovered that in addition to one rumored victim I had known about for years, there had been another victim of Drake's sexually violent behavior when he and the victim were in kindergarten. Neither of the other victims were able to come forward.

I decided to notify the police. Google found the number of the sheriff's department of my old hometown, and I left a message with the front desk. They said a detective would return my call.

. . .

My phone buzzed in my right pocket. I was between patients at my desk. I looked at the screen.

"RESTRICTED."

It must be the detective. My heart galloped. I walked from the middle of our galley-style physician's office to the back door, grabbed our doorstop (a beaten-up stapler), and propped the back door open.

I swiped the phone to answer as I hurried up the back steps and pressed the phone to my left ear.

"This is Frances Southwick," I announced, cutting the greeting portion of the conversation short.

"Yes, hello, Frances. This is Detective O," the caller responded in a quick, friendly manner. "I'm with the sheriff's department. Is this a good time to talk?"

...

Over the following several months, I detailed the trauma to Detective O and three other police officers, both on the phone and in person.

POLICE REPORT

On 06-06-16 at approximately 1600 hours, I was dispatched to a phone message reference a sex assault that took place in 1997. . . .

On July 07, 2016, I requested an interview of the victim [redacted][39] be conducted by the A. County Police Department. That interview was conducted on July 18, 2016 by Detectives [M. K.] and [N. P.]. . . .

On August 4, 2016 at 14:00 hours I met with the principal at [Rural Town] High School Mr. Rainer . . . for a video recorded interview. I asked Mr. Rainer if he remembered two past students [redacted] and Drake Erebus and he stated he did. I asked if he remembered a report from [redacted] about Drake Erebus and he stated he did however he did not remember the exact date(s) or the time frame. Mr. Rainer said he remembered an incident that happened in a class room at the high school and it happened months before he had become the counselor at the [Rural Town] School District. Mr. Rainer said he did remember an incident but the dates and times were not clear. [Redacted] had reported to Mr. Rainer a sexual violation of her that happened in one of the classrooms at the High School and Drake was the perpetrator and [redacted] the victim. Drake forced himself upon [redacted] and threatened her to do what he wanted her to do or to not say anything or both. The threat was of Drake doing something to [redacted] with a weapon possibly a gun. Mr. Rainer said the incident was a definite sexual violation he would call an attempted rape, sexual harassment or physical violation or a possible rape. I asked Mr. Rainer if he had reported the incident. He

---

39 This refers to me.

stated he had taken notes and [redacted] also took notes but he did not know what had happened to the notes. I asked what the next step was and he stated he contacted [redacted] and Drake's parents. Mr. Rainer said he had a positive relationship with [redacted] and he believed what she told him. He said he thought both students were about 17 years old at the time. Mr. Rainer said he had taken notes but he could not locate them. He said that no one to include Drake ever denied it happened. He said he spoke to Drake's mom Cecelia Erebus said she did not believe a rape had happened. Mr. Rainer said he remembered the parents wanted to keep the two kids away from each other. I asked if he remembered talking to Drake. He stated he was sure he did but did not remember the conversation. I asked Mr. Rainer if he had any additional information and he said he did not have any knowledge that there were any other facts or witnesses in the case. I asked if there were any school records that might be still in existence. Mr. Rainer said he would check and provide them to me if they were found. (See recorded interview for complete information.) . . .

On August 4. 2016 I received an email from Mr. Rainer he wrote he was wrong on the ages of the kids that they were not 17 years old but 14 years old when it was reported.

I was able to contact [redacted] by telephone. They are now living in [Mountain Town]. They did not return my phone calls for several days and when they did they were not very willing to cooperative with me. Both of them claimed to not remember any incident with their daughter and Drake ever occurring. I asked [redacted] if she remembered an incident with the school counselor Mr. Rainer. She said she had almost forgotten that there was a meeting with Mr. Rainer. She said nothing was ever said in that meeting about any abuse and she left not knowing why it was even held. She said she was sorry she was so unhelpful but she did remember going in for a meeting and it seemed uncomfortable because nothing ever came of it and she never pursued it. It may have been something about her daughter getting along in school. I asked if she recalled a student named Drake and she said she did [redacted]. I asked if the police or Sheriff's Office was ever called because of Drake and her daughter. She stated she did not remember [redacted] said she should remember because it was the only meeting they ever had. I spoke to [redacted] and asked if he remembered the meeting and he stated he did not. (Please see recorded interview for complete information.) . . .

I contacted Cecelia Erebus. on the telephone on August 25, 2016. . . .

I immediately called Drake Erebus and left him several messages. He did not return my calls. On August 30, 2016 at 1650 hours, I was contacted on the telephone by Attorney Calvin Boggart. He stated he had retained Drake Erebus as a client on a suspected sexual case. I explained I had never spoken to Drake in person or on the phone about him being a suspect in a case. Mr. Boggart said this was an old case and the statute of limitations was probably past. I requested he and Drake come to my office for an interview. He laughed and said "Only on TV shows like Law and Order do attorneys come in and talk to the police. I explained that many people come in to talk to the police if they don't have anything to hide. This concluded our conversation.[40]

---

40 The excerpted text comes directly from the police record of the 2016 police report by Detective O. To maintain consistency with the rest of the text, all names have been changed. Otherwise, the excerpted text has been reproduced as written; no edits have been made for language or grammar.

GEARING UP FOR TRIAL

"Got something from the DA," I said to Jude as she cruised from the mailbox back to our driveway.

It was June 2017, and we now lived in California. The white envelope addressed to me, with the district attorney's office as the return address, was stuffed between pages of colorful junk mail. I sat in the passenger seat of the Subaru, holding it steady.

"Oh yeah?" she asked.

"Yeah. I bet it's either nothing or a subpoena," I posed.

I opened it.

"It's a subpoena."

When we arrived home, I walked straight to the couch in the sunroom and surveyed the details of the subpoena.

THE PEOPLE OF THE STATE VS. DRAKE EREBUS,
A DEFENDANT
CHARGE: SEX ASSAULT 2-OTHER MEANS EVENT:
JURY TRIAL
THIS WILL BE A TWO DAY TRIAL
You are hereby commanded to appear on 10/25/2017 at 9:30 a.m.

There was a line at the bottom for me to sign, to notify them within ten days that I was aware of the command, and that I would attend the trial, otherwise "we will pursue personal service of the subpoena upon you."

...

"Francie, can I ask you something else?" Becky asked slowly.

She was wiping down our kitchen counters, butcher block wood, and old yellow tiles.

Becky and I were old friends. In college, she was pre-pharmacy (she was now a pharmacist) and I was premed. We had laughed our way through organic chemistry I and II together. We had grown much closer since then. She had been flying out to visit me every month or two.

"Sure," I said.

She stopped wiping but could not quite look me in the eye.

"How are you getting ready for the trial? I mean, I was looking at the statistics."

I paused.

She was right.

I had read them a few nights before.[41]

Sigh.

It was all at once piercing, nauseating, depressing, and . . . not surprising.

Becky stood there in my kitchen, with her gaze on the sponge in her hand. She looked up and met my eyes.

I cannot do more than my part.

---

41 More than half of violent crimes in the United States are not reported to the police, and less than half of those reported are solved (Gramlich 2020). One report (Morabito, Williams, and Pattavina 2019) showed that of 2,887 female victims who reported sexual assault between 2008 and 2010, 544 (18.8%) of the cases involved arrests; charges were filed in 363 cases, and 189 ended in a guilty verdict. Of the guilty verdicts, 152 (81%) were the product of a plea bargain, 7 (3.7%) involved a guilty finding by a judge, and 25 (13.2%) involved a guilty finding by a jury. In 11 cases, a jury acquitted the defendant following a trial. Only 45 (1.6%) of cases reported to the police were tried in court.

I am not in control of the verdict any more than I am in control of what happens to the plastic I put in my recycling container.

"I put it in the recycling bin," I reply.

. . .

Journal entry. November 24, 2017.

For the past few months, I have come back to the same few words every time . . .

Countdown.

Trial.

Anxious.

Jude.

Becky.

Delilah.

It is now November 24, 2017. The trial is December 5 and 6, 2017.[42] Less than two weeks away. So close, I can feel it. And at the same time, four more workdays and seven more off days seems too long. The waiting, however, is much more tolerable when I remember a few things . . .

An astronaut is counting down the days 'til she sees her dog.

A father is waiting to see if his toddler can come off steroids and still live.

A man is waiting to hear if he is one of the next batch of employees to be laid off.

A young woman is trying to wait out her depression, hoping this medication is the one that will make life tolerable.

---

42 The trial was pushed back due to logistical delays.

And I think of all the things I have already waited for. Biopsy results. Organic chemistry exam results. When I was six or seven, waiting for Christmas to arrive was excruciating. These waits have built up my tolerance.

But I still want the trial to be done.

...

Journal entry. November 24, 2017.

Becky and I had our weekly hour-long phone call yesterday. She was walking her Saint Bernard in the on-and-off rain, sometimes taking refuge under a gazebo lit by blue lights, while I paced around half my house. Our niece is visiting, and she and Jude were having a heart-to-heart in the other half of the house.

For months, part of our weekly conversation has inevitably held the heading "Trial." In this week's episode, we discussed what we can do to prepare.

What will we need?

First, we need the actual courtroom.

The date has already been moved once, and we have already driven to the courthouse once. The drive from Becky's house to the courthouse is about thirty minutes. Becky had made a mixtape with both sentimental and hilarious songs. I had found the music emotionally satisfying as we drove to the courthouse. We had walked into courtroom 601 and were promptly asked to leave by the assertive judge who will be presiding over my case. We had walked into her courtroom during another case, and she had not hesitated to interrupt the proceedings, address us directly, and send us away due to the sensitive nature of the case at hand. Because of this, we love her and fear her.

Second, we need sustenance.

The night before, we will have sub sandwiches. I'll pack away as much as I can—extra glycogen for the stress to come. We need snacks, too. Cheese, nut, and fruit snack packs are ideal—some protein and carbs sprinkled here and there to help us glide through the day. Becky still has these from our last visit. I will also need caffeine for the mornings and noontimes of the trial days—carefully measured, so as not to fall asleep or become light-headed.

Third, we need to take care of Jude.

This is intense, not only for me, but for her, too. Jude needs to meditate the night before, but she forgets sometimes. Becky will strategically place her yoga mat in the guestroom as a reminder.

Fourth, we need to check our physical appearance.

Becky tells me she has two irons. She will help iron my two court outfits. She already has purchased her own new court outfits. I don't know what I'll wear yet—probably some boring work clothes. This morning I had a half inch taken off my hair to tidy it up a bit. Jude has been considering how to keep her hair as well; she also wants to make a good impression.

In essence, we are all trying to be on our A game. Good hair, good emotional health, good food, good sleep, good appearance. It's tricky being a woman, going up to be a witness. The key witness. I am again faced with the problem of not appearing to be a dainty victim, yet also not a bitchy man-hater. I say "again" because this comes up so frequently. Interviews, meetings, interactions with colleagues. Professional working women are often labeled as a bitch or a pushover. I also don't want to be in the third common category, "hot girl." Ugh. I know what types of thoughts trickle through the minds of humans.

Weirdly, I don't think Gary has been subpoenaed. I think it's because other than saying how he had hunted with Drake and his father, and maybe describing a panic attack I had near the Home Ec room, he would not be a helpful witness. I think my lawyer can ask me all the questions she normally would have asked Gary . . . and not have to worry about Gary helping the defense.

I am still amazed Delilah is a witness for the defense; however, legally, she cannot decline—she has been subpoenaed.

I'm also surprised Dr. Dolcetti has NOT been subpoenaed. But I suppose she wouldn't provide any new information, really. The defense knows her notes are packed with PTSD details, which is not exactly helpful for them.

In current events, there is an explosion of talk about sexual assault and harassment. The #MeToo movement and the Harvey Weinstein phenomenon are huge. Not ideal for the defense. It's forcing our society to consider the reality of rape culture and how we each contribute to it and/or have been victim to it.

I have a feeling that following through with this trial is one of the most important things I can do. Speak up. And yet . . . I dread the questions from the prosecutor. I know what he's going to ask me.

"What were you expecting? Why would you agree to go to his house to play strip poker?"

And when he asks, he's going to use his male dominance.

I've looked him up online already. He is a registered Republican. He lives in a small mountain town with his wife, who is also a registered Republican. The internet is amazing. I was able to retrace their entire relationship, through law school and everything. His wife is interested in the arts. That's a good sign at least, right? I don't know. However, his web page regarding sexual assault uses terms and phrases such as "slut," "claim they were taken advantage of," and "propensity for promiscuity and untruthfulness."

...

The first time I mentioned the trial to Delilah was forced.

In the summer of 2016, when I reported my experiences, I had asked the detectives to avoid involving my family, but they said their involvement would be inevitable. I was asked to provide Delilah's and Gary's phone numbers, and I complied. To prepare Delilah, so she would not blame me for not giving her a warning, I called to let her know she would be getting a call from the police. I explained why.

"What?! Well, what if he's a good man now? So you want this in the headlines?"

She was anxious and reactive, and I gave her that. It was a lot.

But as the weeks went on, the detectives told me that despite Mr. Rainer's helpful reports and memories of the sexual assaults I reported, Gary and Delilah were both unwilling to cooperate with the investigation. The detectives told me that both Gary and Delilah reported no memories of any problems between Drake and myself and no memories of any communication with Mr. Rainer regarding any type of misconduct, sexual or otherwise.

. . .

"I wanted to bring something else up," Delilah said in her practiced somber tone.

It was August 2017, three months before the trial. My elbow started to sag from holding my phone. She and I had been talking for some twenty minutes, but it felt longer.

My sandals were sticky from the pollen and sap from the neighborhood trees. The sun was shining so beautifully. My legs were tingling pleasantly from walking. (I pace when I talk on the phone.)

"Okay, what's up?" I tensed, knowing it was about the case.

"I had another call yesterday . . . from a police officer. Regarding your . . . case."

I thought for a second.

Yeah, she probably stalled and denied any knowledge, again.

"Oh?" I asked coolly.

"Yeah, it was a different policeman."

"What did the police ask?"

"Oh, the same sorts of things. . . . They wanted to know what I remembered about Drake, and his family, and his relationship with you..."

"Mmhmm."

"Francie, the more I think about this, the angrier I am at Mr. Rainer," she said, her voice escalating a bit. "I mean, here you were, you spilled your whole story to him, opening your whole self, and then what did he do? Nothing! I don't remember that meeting, Francie."

"I thought you just said you did remember it," I replied flatly.

"I came away from the meeting thinking, well, he's a new school counselor, maybe this is just a precaution, or something . . . I was very confused," Delilah said.

"Hm. Well, I remember the meeting. I remember crying, and not being able to speak much."

"You weren't speaking at all!" she reacted.

I gritted my teeth.

You remember the meeting, Delilah.

But I knew why she both remembered and did not remember. I knew why she was defensive. I do the same thing. I alternate between blaming myself and blaming Drake. Blaming Delilah. Then Gary. Rainer. Myself. Drake. Delilah. Round and round goes the blame.

"I remember the car ride home. Delilah, you were upset. You asked whether I was going to tell Gary, or if you were. We got home. I went to my room. Then you came for me and brought me to your bathroom. Gary and you stood there, angry. Or scared. Upset. And Gary scoffed, 'Well, do you want to press charges?' "

"If Gary had known what was going on, he would have [acted physically violent toward] Drake on the spot," Delilah sputtered.

"Yeah, that was one of the two reactions I was preparing for. Maybe that's why I hesitated when he asked if I wanted to press charges. And then he said, 'She doesn't care about herself, anyway,' and then he left for the weekend."

Delilah made a worried noise.

"Delilah, it didn't fit into your schema of your life. You thought, 'Francie and I are so close! She would have told me this before.' Then when Gary blamed me and left, well, I think you blocked it out of your memory."

Silence.

"Yes, that's possible," Delilah finally admitted.

"I think you just couldn't believe it. Literally couldn't. So you put it out of your mind so we could all keep going. But then how was it for me? I had to keep going to school with him."

Silence.

I continued.

"It's a polarizing topic. People have strong reactions to the rape of a family member. There are few options. Most people either blame the perpetrator, blame the victim, or don't deal with it at all. Denial. You chose denial."

Silence.

I ventured back to the topic of Gary.

"You know, he and I *still* have never spoken about it. Even after the letter. He has never even acknowledged he *got* a letter."

Two years prior, I had mailed long letters to Delilah and Gary, telling them about my hospitalization, pointing out why I was upset with them about how they treated me and each other during my childhood, reminding them of the salient parts of my ordeal with Drake, each letter including a long postscript explaining what I appreciated about their parenting, for balance. Gary had not responded.

"You know what he says every time you or that letter comes up?" Delilah asked tearfully.

"What?"

"Well, first, when he got it, he immediately threw it away."

"Yeah, I figured. I still have a copy if he wants it again," I said, knowing this would only ever be a hypothetical situation.

"Yeah. I kept mine. Anyway, whenever the letter comes up, he says, 'She *knows* I don't know anything, that I don't remember and didn't get the story, so why is she holding me to something she knows I don't remember?!" Delilah cried.

Nausea. Gary storming out of the bathroom, through the attached bed-room, down the stairs, out the door.

"You know, memory is a fascinating thing," I offered, steadying myself. "It's so different for everyone. Each person involved in this remembers it differently. And I would like to think, I mean, because I was at the center of all this, and it was traumatic, I'd like to think I have a lot of it right in my memory."

Silence.

"I mean it really is interesting. Memory is a construct, right? Mr. Rainer doesn't remember the meeting, but he remembers trying to work with you and Gary. He said the two of you were totally uncooperat—"

"No. No, no," she interrupted.

"Yeah! Uncooperative. Isn't that interesting?" I asked.

Silence.

"You know, Francie, when you first told me about this, I mean, when I got your letter, I looked through every old picture of you. I was looking to see where I might have missed it. I looked into your eyes in all those photos."

"Yes, you told me you did that, when we met in Pittsburgh," I said.

"Yeah . . ." she trailed off.

Silence.

"Well, if you want to know what I remember about that time, I am working on a book about it, Delilah. I could give you some of it to read," I offered.

Silence.

"I . . . I guess I *have* to read it," she muttered.

"You don't *have* to read it. Last time I offered for you to read this stuff, you said no, remember? You said you were an ostrich, that you bury your head in the sand, and that you didn't want to," I said, trying to sound steady and not angry. "Why don't I just send you the part about the meeting with Mr. Rainer?"

"Okay, yeah, let's start there," she said.

A phrase suddenly echoed in my head.

Tampering with a witness.

"You know, on second thought, why don't we wait until November, when the case is over?" I asked.

"Yes. Yeah, that sounds like a good idea," she jumped on board quickly with that suggestion.

"By the way, did you get a subpoena?" I asked.

"No, I didn't," she replied in a more sober tone. "When is the trial?"

"October 24 and 25, I think."

"Oh . . . that's when my dad's birthday was," she choked.

Silence.

"I . . . actually wasn't planning on telling you the dates of the trial. I don't really think it would be . . . helpful or productive, for you or for anyone, for you to be there," I said.

"Oh. Okay," she whimpered.

I'm hurting her, again.

"At some point, I do want to talk more about another part of that letter," she reminded me.

"Mmhmm, okay, have a good day. Love you, Delilah."

"I love you, too, France."

. . .

A week later, I found myself walking outside again, talking to Delilah about her fishing trip in Alaska with Gary last week.

"How was Alaska?" I asked.

"It was . . . I don't know, France. How was your week?"

"Fine. . . " I answered.

"Okay, Alaska. It was...I mean, it was a fishing trip."

"Yeah, I remember something about bad fishing trips," I said. I felt a twinge in my chest.

"Yep, as long as Gary is having fun, right? He doesn't even notice what's going on with anyone else," she complained.

She was right.

She was also 65 years old, now.

"Francie, I want to tell you something,"

"It was o—"

"Francie, I want to tell you something," Delilah changed the subject.

Yep, back to the case.

"I am going to make myself available at the end of October. I can be in Denver, ready for you, if you need me. If you want me for support, or anything."

I flushed and my nostrils flared.

Yep, back to trying to connect with me again because you feel cut off from Gary.

"Mmhmm," I replied.

"I mean, I want to be as supportive as . . ."

You want to look *supportive.*

"No, thank you for offering—I think it will be better for everyone, including you, if you aren't there," I said.

"Well. I guess you'll have Jude."

"Yeah, Jude will be there, and Jude's brother, and Becky," I said.

And now, I'm the bad guy, again.

. . .

Journal entry. October 8, 2017.

I feel like a horrible daughter.

I feel sick.

I feel anxious.

I feel like I should not be doing this because it's so hard.

Becky's going to call in a minute.

I feel like a horrible daughter because Delilah told me she got served with a subpoena yesterday. They served it in person, not like my mail-in one.

I feel like I'm sinking.

And now the validation, as Dr. Dolcetti would advise . . .

It makes sense that I feel sick, anxious, and like I'm sinking because Delilah is going to have to own up to her past, and that is going to cause her pain.

And it's okay that I am having these feelings. . . . I'm only human, and these feelings are feelings, which means they will pass. It's an emotion, not an emergency.

I've got Jude, Becky, Faith, and Jude's brother.

Delilah, by the way, was subpoenaed by Drake's attorney.

This is so fucked up.

But you know . . .

There are consequences to our actions.

I believe there will be more positive change because of this lawsuit, regardless of the outcome.

Delilah was so anxious. I gave her the names of my attorney, the investigator, and the victim's advocate, and she scribbled them down. I'd like for my team to be able to work with her, if possible. I don't know how all of this works. She says she's "just a citizen," like when she and I went to this same courthouse in 1999, when I wanted to learn what a courthouse really looks like.

I was, and still am, a huge nerd.

Delilah wants to be on everyone's side. She wants to be the face on both sides of the penny, and around the rim, too. I get that. I want everyone to like me, too.

But Delilah has a different level of this trait. She has a hard time asserting an opinion. Her most consistent opinion is "balance," which I often agree with—but sometimes there is a rapist and a victim. I'm not sure if she understands this.

She said the police officer was a woman. The officer asked, "Are you Delilah [surname]?"

Delilah said, "Yes," and the officer said, "You have been served."

...

"I think you *did* come to me," Gary mused.

My eyebrows raised.

I was at home with Jude in early October, two months before the trial, getting ready to have a conversation with Becky, when my phone rang. Gary. He had not called me in over two years.

"Oh?" I asked.

I decided to remain as neutral and professional-sounding as possible, to encourage him to share.

"Yes! I mean, I didn't go and talk with Mr. Rainer. I know that. I never went to that meeting. I remember your mom coming home from the meeting. She seemed confused, like she didn't know why she had been asked to meet with him."

"Mmhmm."

"Yeah. And I remember walking outside the Home Economics room with you. And there was a room just off that Home Economics room. And you were scared. You were worried Drake was going to be there. Do you remember that? Was there something with that Home Economics room?"

He seemed genuinely interested.

I paused.

"Yes, there was an event in the Home Ec room. I'm very happy you are willing to talk about this. And I think we can have a more open discussion after the trial," I answered, calculated.

"I KNEW IT! There was something about that room. And there was a little room off it, to the east. Wasn't there something with that? I knew it!"

I could hear him beaming.

"Well, I'm glad you are up for talking about this," I redirected again, explaining the need for me to remain as impartial as possible when it came to any potential witnesses. I explained that I did not want to be accused of tampering with witnesses.

He understood.

"So is it coming up? When is the trial?"

...

"Will you iron my three potential court outfits?" I ask Becky sheepishly.

The trial is in the morning. Tomorrow.

"Oh my God, Frances, yes!"

Jude and I had flown out from California to stay with Becky and her family in Colorado. They live less than an hour from the courthouse. I have never seen anyone prepare and support another person as much as Becky and Jude have prepared and supported me leading up to my trial. I am exhilarated and a bit tremulous.

"Okay. We got iced coffee, full-strength and light, and we got snack packs for the breaks. We got the mix CD for the car. We are going out to breakfast in the morning to make sure we have plenty of protein in our systems. We got . . ."

She continues to itemize the preparatory steps she has taken for the meetings ahead.[43] (To avoid undue stress when speaking around her toddler and seven-year-old, Becky calls the trial sessions "meetings.")

---

43 Becky had also mailed me a quilt, the entire *Harry Potter* DVD series, art supplies, and numerous supportive cards leading up to the trial, in addition to giving me hugs, sending me emails, giving me calls, and joining me in any-hour-of-the-day-or-night texting sessions.

I grab my garb. Three button-down shirts, three pairs of pants. All work clothes, to keep me focused. All carefully chosen the night before.

"Okay, do you think pink is too much?" I had asked Jude, facing the full-length mirror back in the comfort of home.

She pursed her lower lip and eyebrows with pause.

"No, I think that's a good choice."

"Oh, you know, this is the shirt I was in during the taping."

I had been questioned for a few hours in a police station, over a year ago. The session had been recorded for police evidence. I wondered if wearing the same thing would look suspicious to the jurors.

"Oh well, it's my best shirt," I conceded, folding it into the black travel suitcase.

I agonized over how to wear my hair, whether to wear a necklace, belt, or my wedding ring. Which shoes . . .

How should I walk?

Should I bring my briefcase up to the witness chair?

How should I smile? Should I smile at all?

Should I look at Drake? Oh, God, Drake is going to be there.

Should I look at the jury when answering? The YouTube videos said I should. But it seems so contrived. If I were a juror, would I initially wonder why the witness was looking at me, and then cave to the neuropsychological device of eye contact? Or would I find it creepy and planned?

Becky accepts the blue, gray, and khaki pants, plus the purple, pink, and checkered shirts. She carefully drapes them over her quilting table and plugs in her iron.

...

Journal entry. December 5, 2017.

REMINDER LIST FOR TRIAL

No drinks in courtroom

Watch Fred Rogers video

Briefcase

Review details of events

Black pen × 2

Silver top lip balm

Water (once we get there)

Cell

Charger

Mixtape

Extra iced coffee (for noontime)

Snacks

Jude—meditation

Sit up

Speak clearly

Take break if needed

THEY KNOW NOT WHAT THEY DO

In reality, however, [the] legal system . . . may be indifferent or hostile to her. . . . Just as her life is stabilizing, a court date is likely to revive intrusive traumatic symptoms. The decision to seek redress from the justice system, therefore, cannot be made lightly. The survivor must make an informed choice with the full knowledge of risks as well as benefits;otherwise, she will simply be retraumatized.

—Judith Herman, *Trauma and Recovery*

Musical Interlude: "Natural Law" by Frazey Ford[44]

Remember, only answer what they ask, Frances. Hold your ground.

I kept my hands where the jury could see them and my posture upright, never leaning back in the chair. My chin was tucked down. My face was bright and alert but not pleased.

Mr. Boggart, Drake's defense attorney, did not start by pacing around in front of me, the way the YouTube videos said he would.

He stood behind a small wooden structure I would usually call a podium or lectern. He rolled his eyes at the jury and huffed when I asked

---

44 The lyrics found online often misquote Ford; please listen to the song closely.

him to rephrase questions. He asked about sexual tension. He asked for details about Drake's anatomy, and mine. He smirked, sometimes shifting his weight onto one leg coyly. He used alternating cadence, fast and slow. He alternated between appearing concerned and annoyed, on my side and on attack. He presented me with an exhibit, a fictional sketch of Drake's basement. He had to admit it was false when I probed.

For six hours he worked me on every detail and every angle he could.

I wondered to myself frequently, Is it a good thing to keep my head about me?

Should I simply let myself feel, so the jurors see it? What am I supposed to do here?

The media applauded Andrea Constand for holding herself together so well. People respect women who look tough, right?

Or would they understand the situation better if I allowed my feelings to come through? But if I let them come, then I may not be able to continue.

The judge clarified the pieces of testimony that were and were not admissible. The jury was not permitted knowledge about the other alleged victims, or the years of abuse before the statute of limitations timed out, or Drake's pattern of violent language and behavior. They were not privy to his fantasy of his own death: sexually assaulting a woman, then performing a high-mortality act of domestic terrorism, then ending his own life.

The jury could not hear about how Delilah had been scared of him when he was a child, or how my family had feebly attempted to protect me by putting me in kindergarten at age four, keeping me a year ahead of him in school, or how Gary had hurt Delilah, or how Delilah had abused me.

The jurors were selected via four hours of screening, and all those who had been affected by sexual abuse were eliminated from the jury pool. In other words, the jurors were required to be people who knew next to nothing about the subject matter at hand.

. . .

Journal entry. December 6, 2017. Written while sequestered, after I had given my testimony.

I realized something. . . . When I was unsettled with my memories and myself, I couldn't feel safe alone, because the memories would begin crowding in, stealing all the fun and energy and safety I used to feel while being alone. Now I am sitting alone in this juvenile room and I am feeling freedom, wondering if this is a lasting freedom or if my brain will eventually seize again, forcing me against myself.

. . .

Becky and I sat on a couch in the small, cozy lobby of the district attorney's office. We were a few floors up from the courtroom, waiting for the verdict.

Jude and Faith were down in the courtroom, waiting for the jury to return.

"It'll probably be a while," Becky said.

"Yeah," I agreed.

Becky pulled a book out of her backpack while I pulled a sketch-pad out of mine. I curled my right leg under me and sat on it. We sighed and tried to ignore what we were waiting for.

Every once in a while I would look up and we could not help but share a smile. We had done all we could do. The judge had even told the courtroom (without the jurors present) that the district attorney had proven their case.

Ten minutes later Becky got a text from Jude saying they were coming up. I scrunched my eyebrows down and paused my breath.

Coming up?

Becky's smile fell flat. She was not breathing, either. I stretched my mouth to the right, bit down, and tore a little piece of the inside of my left cheek with my canines.

The door opened.

For half a second Jude was stoic and smiling. Then her eyes found mine, and her words helplessly tumbled out.

"Not guilty, honey, it's not guilty. I'm sorry, babe," she said as she leaned forward, her legs not carrying her toward me as quickly as her will to comfort me.

WHAMMMMMM.

Then, quiet.

Faith, Becky, Jude, the victim's advocate, the detective, the two district attorneys all eyed me with tented brows.

I smiled broadly, raised my hands gently in front of me, gestured to the coffee table, and said, "But look who is on the cover of *TIME Magazine.*"

The cover belonged to the people of the #MeToo movement who had imprisoned Harvey Weinstein and Bill Cosby.

"This is a win. We have—"

I slumped rapidly, landing on Becky's torso.

"Call 911!" the victim's advocate cried.

"No, no, wait, this is—" Jude said.

"Her cataplexy. This happens, so—" Becky interrupted.

I could hear, but the room was dark and distant. My eyes were half open.

Jude swept toward me, taking hold of my shoulders and head, and Becky moved out of the way. Jude leaned my back against her chest.

I thought about the ride that morning to the courthouse, blaring music and dancing ridiculously in the car with Jude and Becky, then pulling up to the courthouse. I had reminded everyone that the jury members could be anywhere. We were poised from then on.

I thought about how Delilah had asked Becky if I had seen her talking with the Erebuses in the hallway. Delilah was concerned it might have looked bad.

I thought about Drake, sitting with his arms crossed and his legs open, glaring at me while I was in the witness stand.

I thought about Becky's kids back at her place. Jay was probably putting mac and cheese on the stove.

I thought about Drake and me walking around the block, at the four houses, when we were kids, and when we were thirteen.

I thought about the last pediatric patient who had come to me after a sexual assault. I had given her a little yellow plastic ring with googly eyes.

I thought about Drake's lawyer, asking me in a gentle voice if he could take a sip of water after he asked me if I remembered Drake's pubic hair.

I thought about the giant Snickers bar my old rural town friend Faith had brought for me today. Was it just one huge Snickers bar, or were there little Snickers bars in there?

I thought about Drake's two other alleged victims I knew of by happenstance. I wondered how many others there were, and how many more there would be.

Gradually my strength returned, starting with my eyes, then my mouth, then my back. I shuddered and yawned, and my extremities curled up, then slowly stretched. My jaw chattered, the final step before I could stand. I looked at Becky and Jude and nodded my head.

Becky ducked under my right arm, Jude supported my left side, and I stood and swung my right foot in front of the left. Faith took door-opening duty. We ambled to the elevator.

"I understand what Jesus meant," I said.

My three supporters halted, eyes fixed on one another.

"They know not what they do. The jury has no idea what they just did."

Musical Interlude: "Weather Pattern" by Frazey Ford

. . .

Becky drove us away from the courthouse on the third and final day of the trial, [45] as she had the other two days. Jude was in the back, and I was in the front passenger seat. I was weak from the cataplexy episode after the verdict. We were pretty quiet.

Becky stared at the road and shook her head.

"It's not right. But things are going to get better. I will teach my kids never to get into that situation."

WHAMMMMMM.

My chest split.

Her plan is to teach her kids not to be like me. If she can't understand after all these months and all this preparation and processing that it wasn't about a mistake I made, then I can't see how anyone will ever understand. It is hopeless.

---

45 If you remember the information from the subpoena, then you have an extraordinary memory! It was scheduled to be a two-day trial, but it was extended.

I wanted to die, and I said so.

Becky looked at Jude.

She drove us to a Red Robin, where the three of us huddled, waiting for a table.

My instinct was to remain completely silent. I knew the relationship was probably over. Becky would not be able to understand.

But after some internal debate, I decided to say some things before I never saw her again. As I cried, I forced myself to say my thoughts aloud.

"I understand if this is the last of our friendship, because it often is, once it gets this hard."

"Goddammit, Becky."

"I didn't do anything wrong."

"I really do understand, Becky. You have to maintain the illusion of safety so you can stay sane raising two girls. But you cannot keep them safe."

I explained that kids spend time one-on-one together. Kids explore sexually, and that is healthy and part of development. I spoke about how it had felt to live with post-traumatic memories and sensations, how it felt to receive blame and judgement from those I love, how the responses and actions of Drake, Delilah, Gary, and Mr. Rainer had caused such damage. I added how I was grateful for Mr. Rainer's support now, and for Becky's support, but if she could not understand at a fundamental level that I was not to blame for being sexually assaulted, our relationship would be doomed to crumble, whether immediately or gradually.

I could not meet her eye as I spoke, but I noticed her red cheeks and shaking body. Though I had not been hungry in weeks, my appetite grew back as I unloaded. I mindlessly ate mozzarella sticks and chicken wings.[46] By the end of my spontaneous monologue, Becky was speechless.

---

46 See the "Narrative" section of Appendix E.

We stood after the meal and wandered toward the car in single file, Becky in front of me. My feet rumbled in slow rhythm across the carpet of the restaurant. I kept my hands stuffed in my pockets to avoid them flopping at my sides, as I was still weak. I pushed my speed to catch her. My first two fingers slowly reached up and tugged twice at the back of her sweatshirt. She stopped, turned, and completely embraced me.

"I'm not going anywhere," she said.

My neck relaxed, and my mouth fell softly onto her shoulder.

A POEM FOR MY LOVE BY JUDITH AVERS

Musical Augmentation: "Fireflies" by Judith Avers

There is no part of you I would change.

no secret sighs behind your back or to your face

things I can't bear—ways I can't stomach

there is no change i would make to our path to NOW.

no boulder i'd skip over; no turn i wouldn't take

no "something" or "maybe" or "if only"

I don't count flaws or pick apart our words

our truth-telling suits me just fine, thank you.

The journey to watch you become you

and me become me

(not new versions, i guess—just different)

has been rocky and deep

and occasionally graceful and swift.

this person you are—is perfect

is layered and complex

mysterious and predictable

knowing and constantly surprised.

this person you are

is the witness to all of the love I can hold.

i stretch out my hands

and give it to you.

i fold my hands over yours and whisper..

thank you.

over and over again

thank you.[47]

---

47 My wife, Judith, wrote this poem. Her writing this poem and giving it to me is an example of practicing love and appreciating realness (Brown 2012).

THE HOUSE, PART 4

. . . Salman, Jude, and Dr. Dolcetti found my body in the opaque room by feel. They swam in through a broken window, grabbed my arms, and pulled me out to safety.

I slept on the street or on the porches of other homes for a while, usually Jude's.

One day I returned home and opened the bedroom door, and the familiar slime sloshed out onto my shoes. The smell was hardly bearable, and the sludge was freezing. I hadn't noticed the smell before, but it must have always been there. I waded in. I was up to my neck in freezing blackness, shivering. The lights were out. I had only a wind-up flashlight, and I mostly had to feel about with blind hands. I remembered the layout of the room, which helped. On hands and knees, I found a gun under my bed, a dead cat in my closet, a knotted garden hose slung over one of the posts of my bed. Miraculously, I found a working video camera and played back the tapes, writing out the story of what had happened.

Suddenly inspired, I called out the window for buckets, and to my surprise, Jude, Dr. Dolcetti, my friends, and the police brought them. We formed a line and began collecting the darkness and dumping it into a large container. We peered into the container to find clear water. Simply picking it up in buckets as a team seemed to be filtering it some-how. I saw the room needed no stain remover because the darkness was now water. It fed the carpets, which had turned to moss, majestic trees, and flowers. The room was healing itself as we collected the liquid and poured it into this huge glass container. I saw a small spigot at the base of the container, filled a cup, and tasted it. It was pure and delicious.

A few days later I tasted it again—it was bitter, with particles at the bottom. I paused and realized that I was alone in the room, the tapes were playing on a loop, and I had no paper. I called for Jude, who walked in. The particles disappeared within seconds. It seemed that the trick was to have people I love in the room, watching my progress.

The more I remembered this, the purer the water got.

Sometimes I can't stop myself. I can't believe the magical transformation. Sometimes I must prove the room was once full of unbearable sludge. I close my eyes and lay face down, my nose and mouth in the healthy stream that feeds the beautiful new landscape of the home . . . California redwoods and poppies with magnolia bushes. Quickly it turns from water to tea-colored fluid, then it thickens and becomes foul-smelling. It fills my pockets and mats my hair. It rapidly rises, forcing me to sit, then stand. Again I call for friends and show them the darkness. Just as before, it becomes fresh water.

Hearing tales of other rooms that have flooded helps me remember to keep friends nearby. Learning of others creating huge community reservoirs of fresh water from their darkness inspires me to keep playing the tapes, writing the story, collecting the water.[48]

---

48 "Shame derives its power from being unspeakable. . . . If we speak shame, it begins to wither. . . . Language and story bring light to shame and destroy it" (Brown 2012).

PEACH TREE

You can't please everyone. But that's okay because
you're not for everyone. It's okay to just be for
these people over here.
These ones who "get" you.

—Allyson Dinneen, *Notes from Your Therapist*

Musical Augmentation: "Revolutionary Love" by Ani DiFranco

Have you ever seen clusters of two-toned orchard trees? It looks
like they have been sprayed for some kind of pest around the bottom.
But then you look again. It is not only the color that is different, the top
versus the bottom; the texture and diameter are mismatched, too.

Why are they like that? Here is the secret. They used to be
two different trees. That's right. They are hybrids. Not pollinated
to be hybrids, but physically cut and Frankenstein-ed. I did not
believe it at first. But it is real. I looked it up. The process is aptly
called "grafting." It is a way to harness one tree's root system hardi-
ness and another tree's fruits or nuts (University of California, n.d.).
Here is how it works. Trees are planted in an orchard and grown to a
certain size, then they are chopped down, approximately a foot above

the ground. The remaining root system is called the "rootstock." Then a smaller treetop, the "scion," taken from another tree in another orchard, is grafted to this root system. Special grafting wax and/or tape is applied to hold them tightly together, and the two amputees get acquainted and grow into a single tree (Csanyi, n.d.). The last plum you ate may have come from the scion of a plum tree grafted onto the rootstock of a *peach* tree.

. . .

My arms are twisted around my shins and thighs. Lump in my throat, tingling in the right side of my face.

Jude is hovering nearby, exhausted. She is a kind wife. She sips up the last drops of patience and energy she has for the day, and she sits and waits for me to feel my feelings.

"I feel like an orchard tree," I say.

I am being adopted. It is controversial, even in my own mind and heart. I am not an orphan. My biological father, mother, and brother are living. But we do not mix. We do not lift each other up.

The estrangement has evolved over the years. Plenty of folks go through painful times with their immediate family members. I know this is not unique to me. Though obviously the details are layered and complex and involve a multitude of opposing values and viewpoints in the making, myriad moments have hacked away at our connection.

Becky began the adoption process. She moved herself, her husband, her two kids, and her Saint Bernard over 1,000 miles to be near Jude and me. A year and a half later, Becky's father agreed to adopt me.

Discord is inevitable in every meaningful relationship. It is about *the recovery and the growth* of the individuals and the connection, the deepening of the love and respect. It is about the rebound. It is about attunement.

Becky hurt me, then she attuned. She stuck it out. She grew with me.

I am a plum scion. I have grafted myself to peach rootstock, and I am applying the wax.

Musical Finale: "One Voice" by The Wailin' Jennys

BIOLOGICAL FAMILY POSTSCRIPTS

DELILAH AFTERMATH

Musical Augmentation: "45" by Judith Avers

I was not able to sit in on other testimonies, so my supporters (Becky, Jude, Michael, Faith, and Mr. Rainer) graciously assisted by telling me what they could remember about the trial, both immediately after the trial and a few years later.

Regarding Delilah, the team gave the following statements:

Delilah's involvement in the trial was a complete betrayal of everything that it means to be a parent. She should have been testifying on Frances's side or absolutely not at all. I strongly feel that it was her testimony that made it easy for the jurors to vote "not guilty." I do recall feeling a lot of confusion, mixed feelings, bewilderment, and sadness from her when we met with her. I [remember] hoping she would refuse to answer some of the questions while on the stand and being so disappointed in her as a human being when she instead answered.

She is broken. She has been broken most of her life. She did not protect you when you were a child and did not protect you at the trial. Delilah had different priorities as a mom. She needed you to be her best friend when you needed a mother. She has been both the victim of abuse and an abuser. . . . She needed to protect her image when really she was protecting her past.

I mostly remember her mannerisms—she looked so uncomfortable and irritated. It was evident that she did not want to be there. [To] every question she was asked, she responded in an annoyed way—most of the time with "I couldn't say," or "I don't remember," or "not that I can say." She looked stiff.

She looked gaunt and stressed. She was very condescending to Frances's attorneys. [She] seemed very annoyed at them and combative with her responses. She was mildly distant with his [Drake's attorneys] but the weirdest [thing] to me was how Frances's attorneys felt like the "bad guys" to her. Very confusing. I was riddled with fury and staring at her so disappointed and trying to make eye contact. I know that she was upset—she started sobbing as she left the room. We were all dumbstruck.

You know, everyone else that testified stayed in the courtroom after they were released from their subpoena—they showed their support for you. The fact that your mom did what she did was [expletive], but when she got off the stand and was told she was released, she grabbed her jacket and stormed out. She couldn't look anywhere near us. Honestly, that was the hardest moment for me—I watched her walk out on you. It was dismissive and cruel. It felt like all of the credibility you had worked so hard to achieve was blown apart right then and there.

...

On December 8, 2017, the last day of the trial, I sent a group text to Gary and Delilah from Becky's car while she drove us from Red Robin to her house. I said:

I know we were very emotionally charged yesterday. I sometimes feel crushed by the weight of indifference and inaction in the face of crystal-clear injustice. Sometimes people just cannot cope with truth. I know this through and through. That you two cannot cope with some truths. I wasn't able to for years. I know you both remember. You may have repressed that period in time, but you remember somewhere. You two are part of the culture who acquitted Drake. And that culture and generation gave rise to my generation, which is standing up to these atrocities in a whole new and authentic way. In 50 years, we will look back at the cruelty of publicly questioning a victim for six hours about the veracity of her information while allowing the perpetrator the option of not even testifying. We all know who was actually on trial here. It didn't have to be this way.[49]

...

On December 8, 2017, Delilah texted me separately, saying, "You are right," and, "I did nothing to help your case." She called herself naive, and said the lawyers rushed her too much. She said she hoped the trial would not interrupt or damage the progress I had made in therapy. She said I could be proud of myself and those in my generation fighting for change, and that she would "never get over failing" me.

I responded explaining that I was exhausted, that I had no strength to forgive at that time, and that I was acutely struggling to recover from the trial.

...

On the morning of December 13, 2017, I texted Gary and Delilah:

We can all get through this. We just have to face it and feel the feelings, and sometimes that takes a while, but it doesn't last forever. This is not the first I have mentioned any of these things. I have told you. You just didn't care or couldn't cope. . . . I have relationships with you each separately. . . . So I have never told you both simultaneously. But now there is hopefully no confusion. And the ball is in your court.

They did not reply.

...

49 Some minor grammatical adjustments were made to the original text messages for enhanced readability.

On the evening of December 13, 2017, I began feeling desperate for Gary and Delilah to reply, so I texted them a goofy thirty-nine-second-long video clip of me as a preteen, along with the message:

This is me, a few months before or after the main incidents. Do you think this child is to blame? Please think about it. . . . Is it more important to be hurt that your actions were called out, or to be there for someone you love?

They did not reply.

. . .

On the night of December 13, 2017, my filter broke. I shared my pain with Delilah separately. I texted:

I am not able to try not to hurt you anymore. I am hurting so much. . . . What I believe is that you still don't understand that you sexually abused me. You don't get it. And so you transferred that defensiveness and disbelief into your testimony, regarding this unrelated event. I think that is the only rational explanation. . . . I think it's either you deal with these things, or we don't have a relationship.

It wasn't until I found out about your testimony and the defense's closing argument and the verdict that I emotionally was crushed by the trial . . .

Let me know when you are stable with a therapist and I will send you the writing about all the events. I still love you.

. . .

By December 14, 2017, I was panicking. I was losing them. I texted Gary and Delilah in a group text:

Please respond, to make sure you both have all of that.[50]

They did not respond.

...

And then, for the first time, Delilah sought out a therapist. On January 1, 2018, she texted me:

I would like to start the new year letting you know I am working hard with a professional on myself. For me and for you.

---

50 I later read, and still work to accept, this wonderful quote from Allyson Dinneen: "It took me a long time to realize that healing doesn't mean I'll be strong enough to put up with anything—it's that I no longer want to be a person strong enough to put up with anything" (2021).

ESTRANGEMENT FROM JAMES AND GARY

Shame, blame, disrespect, [and] betrayal . . .
damage the roots from which love grows. Love can only survive
these injuries if they are acknowledged, healed, and rare.

—Brené Brown, *The Gifts of Imperfection*

Musical Augmentation: "You Don't Know" by Brooke Annibale

In February 2021, my only biological sibling, James, described himself on LinkedIn as a project manager, faithful husband, blessed father, and sinner forgiven.

James has limited space in *Prognosis: Fair* because he and I were rarely close. We had a few moments of connection in college, but overall, the sticking points in our relationship have been many.

James's response to my coming out with diagnoses of depression and PTSD (with no mention of any abusers, their names, or relationships to me) and my hospitalization was that he felt "sorry for our family" and concerned about what pain this might cause Delilah. (Interestingly, I had disclosed nothing about Delilah's inappropriate behavior.)

I explained it had been an olive branch, an attempt for us all to be authentic with one another. He would not accept this.

=ng person, including that I should become technically or academically skilled and financially independent so I would never have to depend on a man, he also told me on many occasions that no one cares about my problems.

I am grateful for many things from Gary; however, he and I share no discernable interests.

Jude, having grieved the deaths of her sister, mother, and father, understandably wanted to help me achieve reconciliation with Gary. She had been texting with him without my knowledge and waited until the final day of the trial, when he offered to come to the trial, to reveal the communication. I thanked Jude for all her efforts, but I asked her and Becky to ensure Gary did not enter the courtroom.

Jude rightly believes this impacted the jury's decision, as I had no biological family in the courtroom on my side, on any day of the trial.

Gary has not responded to my emails or text messages since December 7, 2017. Granted, I have pushed him away. And granted, I no longer wish for contact with Gary.

ESTRANGEMENT FROM DELILAH

Musical Interlude: "Wise Up" by Aimee Mann

Delilah is my mom, and she was the closest person to me for many years. I wanted to continue to connect with her. But gradually over the years, as I cared incrementally more about myself and understood the true dynamics between us, I tapered communication with her from daily to weekly to biweekly to monthly, then eventually to never.

While maintaining a relationship with Delilah, I dreaded our talks. I enjoyed them while we connected, but then I was out of commission for hours or days afterward. Cataplexy, migraines, slowed thinking, slowed speech, disrupted sleep and appetite, and self-injury ensued. Then hours-long talks with Becky, Jude, and/or a therapist to process what Delilah said or did not say.

We tried all types of levels of contact. She visited me and I visited her; neither were functional experiences. I tried having her stay at a hotel or guest house when she visited. We tried combinations of company: Jude/Delilah/me, Gary/Delilah/me, James/Gary/Delilah/me, Delilah/me. We tried email only. We tried mailing a journal back and forth. We both went to therapy. We tried walks and talks on the phone once every couple of months.

We tried every strength, formulation, dose, frequency, and quantity of interaction I could think of, none of which has been successful. It has been absolutely heartbreaking for me.

Several times between 2015 and 2019, I had long talks with her, explaining how much I loved her, but that for my own health, I had to let her go, and I asked her not to contact me.

A few times she gently edged back in. Once with an email about her long-term illness. Another time by mailing me my elementary and junior high school work. Another time she told me she was seeing a therapist.

On December 4, 2018, Delilah sent me an email: "After reading *Trauma and Recovery* . . . I have a better sense about traumatic events and the scars they leave . . ."

Delilah was able to acknowledge the part she played related to Drake. But she was not able to acknowledge that she was sexually inappropriate with me. She projected the responsibility of the acts and the meaning of them onto me. Her email also said: "You took on the role of comforter so seriously. . . . I remember you from a very early age wanting to be a healer. I remember that many times you offered up your comforting touch to those who were hurting."

She admitted she remembered the meeting with Mr. Rainer, both on the phone before the trial, and in notes after the trial.

In addition, her email said: "I am sorry I did not take the meeting with Mr. Rainer more seriously. . . . I dropped the ball."

She was not able to accept true responsibility for her actions and testimony during the trial. She continued to blame others for the way she behaved on the stand: Mr. Rainer (he did not call the police), Drake's attorneys (they told her to keep her answers short and not elaborate), Drake's private investigator (he said Mr. Rainer did not remember, thereby paving a path for her to say she did not remember), me (I should have prepared her), Drake's family (they said they did not remember), and the district attorney (they did not call for an interview).

The last bidirectional communication Delilah and I had was in February 2020. After she and I talked on the phone for an hour, I fell into the pattern of dissociation with the overwhelming urge to self-injure. This day was, for some reason, the final straw. I texted her that I cared for her so much, that I wanted the best for each of us, and that for my health, I could not have contact with her.

Regarding reconciliation, some therapists, well-meaning people, and even Delilah and I have quipped, "you never know," "don't burn bridges," and "maybe someday."

In her final email to me on December 27, 2019, Delilah said: "I never stop hoping one day there will be a reckoning for us. . . . That we all . . . see each . . . other through grace."

I honestly believe that Delilah and I each did the best we could to hold onto each other, and that we parted on mutually understood terms. However, for me, leaving that door open is like hopefully awaiting an abusive ex-partner's return, either hoping they will come to apologize, or sacrificing part of myself to restore the relationship.

The thing is, no matter what Delilah does or says, and no matter how hard I work on myself and the connection, too much damage has been done for us to reconnect. Too much pain, too much betrayal, too much.

The relationships I keep in my life have evolved from what I can survive to what I can tolerate to what is good for me. She said she loved me, but her actions undermined her words.

Musical Interlude: "Winter Coat" by Karen Savoca

. . .

Journal entry. August 2, 2021.

It has been a year and a half since I last spoke with Delilah. Tension has been fluctuating within me. Should I maintain the boundary? Should I call her? What should I do?

This week I worked on building my family tree through the genealogy company Ancestry.com.

Becky's mom is visiting from Florida this week.

Today I read an article by Cheryl Strayed about estrangement.

This evening Jude and I watched a show called *Gunpowder Milkshake*. In the first episode was a scene of a daughter screaming "Mom!" in slow motion as she was being restrained and her mother drove away. I was shaking and weeping. My body could not take it anymore.

I had to call Delilah.

I asked Jude for her number.[51]

I paced in the backyard while Delilah and I talked for an hour and fifty-nine minutes.

It was tense at first. We caught up on facts. She answered my questions about our family tree. She said James now has five kids.

She mentioned that she and Gary are moving back to their hometown to be near people they can call in a crisis.

We also talked about the trial.

Delilah used to quickly end conversations about the trial by saying, "Someday we will talk about my side."

Her side has now been discussed.

---

51 I had blocked and deleted Delilah's number in February 2020, when I decided to cut contact with her.

She initially defended herself by saying that the lawyers I "hired" never called her. I explained that I had not hired lawyers. I said that the charges were criminal. It was the State of Colorado versus Drake Erebus.

It was not Frances versus Drake, nor Drake versus Delilah, nor Frances versus Delilah, nor the State of California versus Delilah.

Since the day of the Columbine massacre, it was about public safety—not Delilah.

I told Delilah the main reason Drake was found not guilty.[52] The jurors said they could not imagine how any mother would forget about their child being sexually assaulted.

"What mother could?" I posed.

Before she could respond, I offered an answer.

"The kind who was trained as a child to ignore any pain or negativity. The kind who was taught to pretend unpleasant things do not exist."

I did not have the stomach to add, "The kind who cannot face that she sexually abused her child."

She tried to explain how she could not have helped; she had not been asked.

"Your chance to help was when the police called you," I said.

She hesitated. I told her I have the police report stating that she and Gary were uncooperative.

She finally conceded. She finally got it. She said she betrayed me. She said she didn't feel like she deserved the title "Mother." She said she could not stomach that word.

She didn't cut me off, interrupt me, or minimize my pain or emotions.

---

52 I learned this information firsthand from those directly involved in the legal proceedings.

She cried.

She apologized.

I said, "I forgive you."

And I meant it.

APPENDICES

APPENDIX A:
THE MOST IMPORTANT APPENDIX

Four years after the trial I asked a handful of my closest supporters for their thoughts about the trial. Here is one response, abridged and lightly edited for grammar:

Frances,

I wish I could have talked to every jury member for their perspective. I want to know what prevented them from convicting Drake. I wish I could have told them more about you.

The trial was almost like a dream. I am rarely anxious, but I was very anxious in the time building up to my turn to testify. Then the time testifying went so fast. I wanted to slow things down and make sure the judge and jury knew the truth and the effect the truth had (has) on you. I have testified in cases before, but never one where the stakes were so high. I so deeply care about you and did not want to let you down—again.

Before the trial I had you frozen in time. I remembered you as a brilliant, innocent girl in high school and that your innocence was stolen from you. I had not seen you in decades. After the trial I saw you as a brilliant survivor. I still see the innocence in you. You are so wise, and so much smarter than me. Your soul has been broken, but not beyond repair. I admire you now more than ever. When you were in high school I wanted to wrap my arms around you to protect you, and I should have done so much more to help you. Now I see you as courageous, hurt, and deeply introspective. And I see that your purpose is linked to helping others who have been victims of rape and sexual abuse.

[I have] guilt over not contacting the police at the time. I trusted your parents to take action, and I should not have. I should have done more myself, and this haunts me to this day. Sadness for how your life has been impacted. And a deep, deep admiration for your courage.

My fading memory has lost many of the specific details about you in high school. But I have shadows and impressions that will never fade. You were (and are) brilliant. I was immediately impressed by how articulate you were, how you were mature and wise beyond your years. You were energetic and full of life. And yet, there was a vulnerability about you. After getting to know you better, I realize where that vulnerability came from. You were a victim in your own home and in your neighborhood. When others should have wrapped their arms around you to protect you, they instead elevated you to adulthood. I remember your beautiful smile and your witty sense of humor. I remember you as my peer counselor.[53] I wanted you in this role so I could both get to know you better and in some way protect you. The more I was around you the more I figured you were not "out there" or around him. So, my motives were partly self-serving and partly a way to keep you safe.

You were socially conscious even as a teenager. I am sure some of this comes from being so abused and mistreated yourself. You always were so compassionate. You were desperate to get out of that small town. Who could blame you? It is cliché, I know, but you were so ready to spread your wings and get out, but there are burdens you have carried along your journey. I knew you were destined to enter a life of service to others in some way. You were passionate, funny, smart, and gentle. You still are.

I think you graduated in 2001. You gave me a senior picture. The picture is in a cardholder on my desk. It is the first thing I see when I

---

53 At my high school, a student could serve a year as a peer counselor as an elective. Each peer counselor was assigned to assist a teacher or counselor by grading papers, tutoring students, and so on.

start my day at school. You are smiling, and the photo captures your brightness and innocence perfectly. It reminds me of you and of my role as a protector of others.

I am so sorry. I am sorry I did not do more when I had the chance. At the time I thought I was doing the right thing by talking to your parents and Drake's mom. It was right, I guess—but it was not nearly enough. I should have taken this to the sheriff, to social services, to any legal entity that would listen. I regret this more than any single event in my life. My other regrets revolve around not keeping in touch with people. Yet not doing more for you at the time affected you in ways I did not anticipate. Why did I not see this? This question still haunts me to this day. Having a chance to state my regrets personally to you and at the trial has helped to spill out some of my guilt, but it has not removed the albatross around my neck. I adored (adore) you. How could I not do more? This story is not about me. It is about you and the pain you have endured, how you have survived, and the triumph of your soul. It is also about your grace.

I hope you are content in your life. Judith seems amazing and [to be] an incredible source of love and support for you. You have helped countless people in your career in the medical profession. You have gone on to live a life of purpose and saved the lives of others. You will continue to save others by sharing your life's story. You are a remarkable woman.

There are life lessons [from the trial] that shape me to this day.

Lesson #1. As an educator, I am given tremendous responsibility that I have never taken lightly. I became an educator largely to teach and protect children. In this area I feel I failed you. I could have done so much more. I have always believed you and trusted you. At the time I felt that informing your parents was the right thing to do. It was. But I should have done more. I should have contacted the sheriff and social services. I should have pushed for the justice you have never received. I regret this. It impacts every decision

I make. However, it does not take away my guilt. It is the biggest regret I have in all my years as an educator. I know you have forgiven me—I have not yet forgiven myself.

Lesson #2 is the power of forgiveness itself. Your grace has empowered me. As I have mentioned, I am still struggling to forgive myself. Guilt is a powerful thing (I was raised Catholic, you know). I can forgive others before I forgive myself. Forgiveness is a gift of grace, and it is the most powerful quality we are blessed with.

Lesson #3. Memory is fleeting. I am getting up there in years, and my memory is fading at times. I write notes now for most any conversation I have. I have always struggled with details, and instead I have sought the meaning and big picture. But details matter, too.

[Lesson] #4. I cannot always fix things. It is my nature to fix problems. I usually can, but I need to admit sometimes I cannot fix everything and need to reach out more often for help.

[Lesson] #5. The justice system is not always just. Mercy is up to us, and it is hard.

It would mean the world to me to stay connected with you. . . . I want to stay in touch with you like I should have done for years. I can remember clearly where you sat when we talked about Drake and Columbine, and how concerned you were about Drake hurting others. This prompted you to share with me what he had done to you. The office is still the counselor's office, although we tore down the wall behind it to expand it. My office is near [the] circle drive. So much changes and so much stays the same. When I became the counselor . . . I told my wife I would leave after the first year or two. Then came the elementary principal job followed by the high school principal position. Two years has become 24. How did that happen?

When it comes down to it, my job/profession/vocation is all about kids. It is about you. I see you now in every student that needs my help and protection. I let you down, and you have lifted me up.

I earlier stated that before the trial, your childhood image was frozen in time. If I close my eyes I can see you in my office. But you are not frozen in time, and now I see an extraordinary adult. You have blessed my life and the lives of others. I love you. I am hoping we can be friends and share our lives with each other. And I hope to see you again soon.

Mr. Rainer

APPENDIX B: HOW CAN WE REDUCE CHILDHOOD TRAUMA?

Momentum is gaining.

Trauma-informed care is at the forefront of medical and psycho-behavioral research, evaluation, and care.

An infamous study by Kaiser correlated the number of adverse childhood experiences (ACEs) to high-mortality diagnoses as adults (Felliti et al. 1998). The study demonstrated a strong correlation between a higher number of self-reported ACEs and health problem diagnoses, and it is a major step in health care toward integrating "behavioral health," trauma, somatic dysfunction, and medical diagnoses.

However, the path to appropriate use of the data from the study is under construction. Trauma experts have voiced concern about the limitations of the study, and the potential for retraumatization via mimicking the study through screening questions about childhood trauma and attempted interventions.

Trauma-informed care involves understanding the links between trauma and disease burden, creating practices and communities to support those who have experienced trauma, and working to reduce the frequency and burden of adverse experiences. One effective approach is using the real-time prevention and intervention model called Safe Environment for Every Kid, or SEEK (Dubowitz et al. 2009). Dubowitz et al. (2009) showed statistically and clinically significant outcomes in terms of the model's ability to reduce violence and neglect of children in the intervention arm of their study. The model screens and provides brief interventions for caregivers at their children's medical visits via a one-page questionnaire, a trained provider, and a social worker (SEEK 2019).

Educating children about their right to safety is also important. I have included a one-page handout for kids called "Dear Young Patient" in Appendix J.

Musical Interlude: "Heaven's Here on Earth" by Tracy Chapman

APPENDIX C: HOW SHOULD WE TREAT A TRAUMATIZED PERSON?

There is no universal treatment for traumatized people.

Renowned body-psychotherapist and author Babette Rothschild highlights this in her introduction to the second volume of *The Body Remembers*:

Facts and sure things do not exist in psychology and psychotherapy. . . . There is no medication or treatment for PTSD that helps more than 50% of clients. This is not a problem in itself as this is consistent in the field of medicine—treatments and medications work for merely a percentage of patients. . . . However, it does become a problem when treatments adopted into the evidence base become misinterpreted or promoted as beneficial for all. (2017)

When a client is ready, as determined by the client and their clinician as a team, the Autonomic Nervous System Table created by Rothschild can be used as a quantitative means to monitor the delicate balance of the therapeutic window. The technique can be adjusted when a patient is either under- or overstimulated. For example, when I transitioned from my standard daily consciousness to dissociation during my sessions with Dr. Dolcetti, we identified a pattern wherein I dissociated at approximately forty minutes into each session, at which point Dr. Dolcetti suggested I stand and get a drink of water from the hall. This act of agreeing to a social suggestion, changing position, ambulating, and swallowing cold water reengaged my ventral vagus, and the dissociation usually subsided.

Bessel van der Kolk exposes the goal of treatment:

And so, the great challenge of our work for ourselves and the people we work with is how do you go inside of yourself and change your brain and change yourself by becoming friends with your internal experience? (2015)

Though some treatments to address trauma include discussing and reporting traumatic events, eager clinicians employing these techniques easily revictimize the client. Focusing on containment and stabilization is critical in early trauma work; this means avoiding explicit exploration of the trauma (Hein et al. 2009).

A two-part approach to patients with PTSD appeals to me. The first part is to consider PTSD a traumatic brain injury (TBI). If we accept that psychology is neurology, then mind = brain, neuropsychological trauma = TBI, and healing from trauma = rehabilitating after TBI.[54] Many aspects of the comprehensive management of patients living with post-traumatic brain injury syndromes are also appropriate for those living with PTSD. I have included a consensus guideline for the treatment of patients with TBI following this appendix.

The second part is choosing and employing a treatment plan. The treatment for patients with PTSD is a nonlinear, dynamic, lifelong dance. Each person's amalgam of history, triggers, relationship status, active diagnoses, and social history is unique, and effective therapists honor each person with attunement, appropriate boundaries, curiosity, validation, and willingness to collaborate.

---

54 Thus, it takes years. The brain has been altered. But it can continue to be altered. Harnessing that truth and focusing on calming and positive experiences to make new neural pathways takes patience and has a significant payoff. When I was discharged from the hospital, Jude's therapist said significant healing would take two to three years. This setting of expectations was helpful for Jude and me. For me, the sign of significant progress was looking forward to time alone in a positive light, rather than dreading what I might think about, read online, obsess over, or do to myself with time alone. It also takes two to three years for one's brain to heal from methamphetamine-related changes and neurogenic pain from certain nerve injuries.

Treatments for trauma generally focus on the following domains: cognitive, micro-physical, macro-physical, or social/environmental.[55]

Cognitive treatments encourage development of insight via exploration and organization of one's experiences. Examples include:

- Acceptance and commitment therapy (ACT)
- Cognitive behavioral therapy (CBT)
- Cognitive processing therapy (CPT)
- Logotherapy
- Narrative therapy
- Prolonged Exposure (PE)

MACRO-physical treatments attempt to regulate internal states and behavior via concrete, active means such as bilateral stimulation, movement, and rhythm. Examples include:

- Eye movement desensitization and reprocessing (EMDR)
- Martial arts
- Somatic Experiencing (SE)
- Yoga

MICRO-physical treatments involve structured self-regulation of internal states at the biochemical level. Examples include:

- Biofeedback therapies
- Meditation
- Psychedelic assisted treatments

---

55 This is a decent but incomplete list of treatments for trauma-related disorders. For a more comprehensive guide, please refer to the "Treating Trauma Master Series" of the National Institute for the Clinical Application of Behavioral Medicine, directed by Ruth Buczynski, and *The Body Keeps the Score*, written by Bessel van der Kolk.

Social and Environmental treatments encourage connection with peers. Examples include:

- Group therapy
- Support groups and networks
- Trauma Recovery and Empowerment Model (TREM)

Many treatments (including the above examples) for trauma integrate two or more domains. Other examples include:

- Animal assisted therapy
- Community-based exercise
- Community gardening
- Comprehensive Resource Model ® (CRM)
- Dialectical behavior therapy (DBT)
- Drum circles
- Music therapy
- Religious and spiritual practices
- Play therapy
- Skills Training in Affective and Interpersonal Regulation (STAIR)
- Stress Inoculation Training (SIT)
- Trauma Affect Regulation: Guide for Education and Therapy (TARGET)
- Theater work

APPENDIX D:
TRAUMA-INFORMED CARE

This appendix is based on the rehabilitation guidelines for traumatic brain injury (TBI) of the Ontario Neurotrauma Foundation (2016) and the guidelines for a trauma-informed approach of the Centers for Disease Control and Prevention (2020).

I created the acronym **SWEPT** as a tool to qualitatively ensure interventions I endorse are trauma-informed.[56] Here is what SWEPT means.

*Patients feel **Safe***. Program providers assess for patient safety via regular inquiries about self-harm and suicidal thoughts and behaviors. When a patient is in crisis, the team assesses the patient's personal support team's capacity for taking on caregiver roles. Supporters are trained to ensure the patient's safety, provide practical and emotional support, look after their own quality of life, and plan respite care.

*Patients feel **Welcomed***. Program team members are educated about trauma, and they mindfully engage with patients. Program team members embody cultural, racial, and gender diversity, aim for equity, and practice inclusion.

*Patients are **Educated and Empowered***. The program educates patients and caregivers about trauma, trauma effects, trauma processing, and community resources (adapted to age, culture, and linguistics,

---

56 Effective programs for patients with post-traumatic disorders are trauma-informed. The basics of trauma-informed care include safety, trustworthiness and transparency, peer support, collaboration and mutuality, empowerment and choice, and attunement to culture, race, and gender.

in both written and verbal formats). Team members fully and sensitively obtain patient consent throughout their assessments and interventions, ensuring the patient is central in setting goals for their own supported and individualized treatment program. Team members provide responsive support based on the patient's dynamic stability and goals.

Patients have access to supportive **Peers and Prepped People**. When appropriate, group treatment with peers and others with similar diagnoses are offered. Program staff, program providers, families, and individuals are mindful of hypersensitivity and fatigue, and they avoid overstimulation (via low sensory stimulation, timely treatment, positive regard, clear and calm communication, clearly marked signage, low question duplication, no questions regarding trauma details, etc.). The program collaborates with community sectors (e.g., police officers, parole officers, emergency medical services, educators, teachers, employers) to expand the circle of trauma-informed interactions.

Patients **Trust the Tortoise**. Processing trauma is a slow activity, like walking a tortoise. Rushing is counterproductive. Therefore, the program provides both acute and maintenance services. The program facilitates a continuum of short-term and long-view patient-tailored goals for cognitive, emotional, behavioral, social, occupational, and recreational autonomy and self-regulation.

APPENDIX E:
WHAT HAS WORKED FOR ME

The following text explores what has been helpful for me personally when it comes to trauma memory processing, but it is not a complete
or one-size-fits-all approach to traumatic memory integration.[57] Much
of what has helped me aligns with approaches from experts in the fields
of psychiatry, psychology, trauma, osteopathic medicine, and physiatry.

A. THE BASICS

The basics include water, food, hygiene, housing, financial stability, exercise, and safety from abusers. For me, safety involved moving
several states away from my abusers and tapering contact with them over
many years.

B. DISTRACTIONS AND BREAKS

Musical Augmentation: "First Aid Kit"
by Judith Avers and Joanna Burt-Kinderman

My initial vision of treating my post-traumatic state was like ortho-
pedic surgery: plan the course linearly, locate and excise the pathologi-
cal section of myself, cauterize the bleeding parts, and sew myself back

---

57 This guide is not meant to be used to diagnose or treat any condition. Every post-traumatic response is different. Individualized neuropsychiatric evaluation and treatment should be
applied by professionals trained in the management of post-traumatic syndromes.

together. I expected resolution in eight weeks. But injured neurons need tender loving care, time, and patience, not scalpels and sutures.[58]

When trauma is touched upon during a therapy session, I need adequate time and space to recover before another session. Over time I have recognized that my therapeutic window of tolerance and efficacy for psychotherapy is approximately twenty-five to thirty-five minutes per session. Beyond this, I tend to dissociate, or otherwise shut down.

Some examples of distractions I use while my brain heals between sessions, and also as maintenance treatment, include: watching *The Golden Girls*, going to the movies, doing puzzles, reading or watching *Harry Potter* or *The Hunger Games*, playing word games, scrolling Instagram, taking walks, and drawing. Having multiple of these options at the ready (e.g., apps on the first page of my phone, pen and notepad in my pocket) and in line of sight makes them more likely to be used. When I am in stimulating situations and when I have time to myself, I play positive music to keep my brain partly occupied and to make intrusive negative thoughts less likely.

C. SUPPORT NETWORK

Incrementally telling my story to supportive people (people who listen to me, people who believe me, people who take my side) and creating a chosen family has been central to my healing process.

"Sharing the traumatic experience with others is a precondition for the restitution of a sense of a meaningful world. . . . Once it is publicly recognized that a person has been harmed, the community must take action to assign responsibility for the harm and to repair the injury. These two responses—recognition and restitution—are necessary to

---

58 For the osteopaths out there—trauma treatment is akin to indirect myofascial release (MFR) and balanced ligamentous tension (BLT), not high-velocity, low-amplitude (HVLA).

rebuild the survivor's sense of order and justice." —Judith Herman, *Trauma and Recovery*

I have slowly recruited a healing network. My wife, Judith, is my number one supporter, and she has been since 2004. Jude literally provided a space for me to keep myself alive while I dove into therapy with Dr. Dolcetti, through the trial, and through the aftermath of my hospitalization and the trial.

Talking to survivors of similar traumas has helped a lot, as has keeping tighter and tighter boundaries to protect myself.

Additionally, working toward greater justice and a more peaceful community is close to my heart, and I connect with people who support social justice causes in a practical manner.

D. AVOIDING TOXIC RECONNECTION

Sometimes I crave reconnecting with Delilah or Gary or James. The familiarity, the loyalty, the shared pasts, the genes all stoke a fire in me to call or text or google or reminisce.

My immediate support network helps me remember what a healthy relationship looks like. A healthy relationship involves me looking forward to interacting with the other person, and feeling better after talking with them. In a healthy relationship, I am willing and able to tell the other person both good and bad news, and I can be my whole self around them. When I remember these things are not possible in toxic relationships, the fire extinguishes.

E. WILLINGNESS AND POSITIVE SELF-REGARD

Through her research, Brené Brown identified three statements associated with freedom from shame: (1) "I am enough," (2) "I've had enough," and (3) "Showing up, taking risks, and letting myself be seen is enough" (2012).

Though at first it seemed impossible, developing and accepting a kind attitude toward myself was key. Fortunately I already had an empathetic attitude toward those I serve; my work involved turning that love toward myself.

It is not helpful for me to simply say to myself, "love yourself," or "get over it," or "the past is in the past." Those statements match my goals of functionality and integration, but I have found it more helpful to approach myself indirectly with a sense of calm kindness, not directives. Though meditation is not a regular practice for me, dialectical behavioral therapy (DBT) and Buddhist principles have allowed me to practice gentle willingness and self-acceptance.

Pawan Bareja, PhD, is a senior assistant at Somatic Experiencing trauma healing trainings, a Buddhist Ritual Minister, and Community Dharma Leader. She practices Vipassana meditation and teaches classes on healing trauma using mindfulness. She writes:

> In my trauma resolution practice, I have found that a powerful way to heal our trauma is to cultivate the four mind states known in Buddhism as the brahma viharas . . . loving-kindness, compassion, joy in the joy of others, and equanimity. We can consciously practice these mind states as part of our meditation practice, and use them to help heal trauma. (2021)

F. LITTLE THINGS

"The capacities for self-care and self-soothing, which could not develop in the abusive childhood environment, must be painstakingly constructed in later life." —Judith Herman, *Trauma and Recovery*

For years I associated pleasure with disgust and shame, thereby creating dissonance and leading me to avoid enjoyable activities. To forge a new path for safe enjoyment, I had to start ridiculously small with pleasurable things I did not associate with disgust and shame, such as lip balm in my pocket, strawberry milk after dinner, a latte after therapy, and a new pen on my desk. I have gradually titrated to other enjoyable activities, such as laying in a hammock in our yard and going to the beach (and actually enjoying it, not just faking it).

G. WORK

My work as a physician has been one of my buoys. Work helps me remember who I am. Engaging others one on one and doing my best to solve logic puzzles and show respect to those seeking care engages me socially, emotionally, and cognitively, and it keeps me going logistically. It is a way for me to feel purpose and meaning.

H. NARRATIVE

"You don't need to try and make it go away. It shouldn't go away. It's just as sad as it ought to be and I'm not going to hide from what's true just because it hurts." —Toni Morrison, *Home*

There was an impressive number of folks Gary "kicked out" of the bank, people who were "worthless," and family members with whom we did not interact, sometimes due to seemingly small offenses. When Gary was presented with a potentially critical or opposing action or word, he often would cut connection with the source.

As young children, identifying and connecting with our caregivers is our means of survival. Shame is an evolutionarily critical emotion that keeps our behaviors in line with those caregivers' expectations.

Shame from sexual abuse is reinforced when we tell our story and receive a shaming response. When we have shame, we must tell our story repetitively in a safe environment to free us from the shame (Linehan et al. 2021). When Gary found out about the sexual abuse by Drake, then told me that I did not care about myself and left the house for the fishing trip, I internalized a massive burden of shame.

As I spoke my truth in a piecemeal way (to Mr. Rainer, then to Jude, then to Dr. Dolcetti, then to a writing group, then to a jury via the trial, then to Becky), I gradually edged away from shame. There was a hiccup in the process (the scene with Becky at Red Robin after the trial), but by that time, I had finally garnered enough strength to push back and educate Becky rather than re-internalize the notion that I was to blame for being sexually abused. As I told her how her words had hurt me and defended my child self, I felt stronger and my appetite returned. Becky was a safe person to practice shedding my shame with. And it brought us close enough to call one another family.

Narrative work is frequently (but not always) part of treatment for those with trauma syndromes. For me, narrative work involves making contact with my memories, writing about them, telling about them, considering them, reading similar stories, reality testing with therapists, and reading literature to understand my past and find appropriate labels for what happened.

I. PAIN TAPER

"Pain. I seem to have an affection, a kind of sweettooth for it. Bolts of lightning, little rivulets of thunder. And I the eye of the storm."
—Toni Morrison, *Jazz*

When Dr. Dolcetti suggested that I do something pleasurable to replace self-injury, I became nauseated. I used to use tattoos to move from painful stimulation to healing, but I only have so much skin and so many dollars. I needed something to bridge from painful stimulation to pleasurable stimulation, something painful but not damaging. Turns out IcyHot works well for this purpose; if more stringent stimulation is needed, holding an ice cube until it melts can help. This is straight out of DBT's TIPP method for regulating acute intense emotion, where TIPP stands for temperature, intense exercise, paced breathing, and progressive muscle relaxation.[59] I also use cinnamon gum, candy, and toothpicks, depending on the situation.

J. CLOTHING AND POSTURE

Comforting clothing and coverings, such as long sleeves, tall socks, hats that cover my ears, sweatshirts, and quilts, are physical shields that also protect my emotional self. I used them liberally during treatment, and I still do.

Postural changes help, too, as Amy Cuddy (2012) explains in her TED talk about the link between physical posture and emotional well-being. When I need to feel safe, I choose between curling up and standing tall. It depends on the circumstance. But understanding that either of these options can be employed as a tool is helpful.

Bessel van der Kolk, Peter Levine (who references Nina Bull's 1951 book *The Attitude Theory of Emotion*), Pat Ogden, Marsha Linehan, Babette Rothschild (and somatic psychotherapy in general), and various texts and series published by the National Institute for the Clinical Application of Behavioral Medicine (NICABM), W. W. Norton and Co., and North Atlantic Books all explore the physical connections among trauma, shame, and body posture. Little body hacks that have helped me either prevent myself from descending into dissociation or extricate

---

59 Marsha Linehan explains how "cold pack therapy" helped during her psychiatric hospitalization, even as it was used as a threat to quell "troublemakers" such as herself: "The cold pack therapy was often a comfort, a means of controlling the demons that roiled me. I sometimes even asked to have the therapy if I felt out of control, if I felt the menacing person [part of me] stalking me and I wanted to stop her" (2020). Like Linehan, I crave some types of intense stimulation. The self-injury urges have calmed, but I had to taper from [overt self-injury methods] to ice cube holding, topical menthol, and capsaicin. Self-injury is common in people who are suffering. When I entered intensive outpatient therapy in Pittsburgh, one of the screening questions was, "Are you self-injuring?" Affirmative answers were so common, stacks of self-injury tracking forms sat on a shelf in the group treatment room.

myself from dissociation include the half smile, opposing my left thumb and index finger gently, sitting at forty-five degrees from therapists and patients, and walking or eating while having conversations.

K. TIME WITH NATURE

"At some point in life the world's beauty becomes enough." —Toni Morrison, *Tar Baby*

Upon hearing of my depression, a friend asked, "You'll be starting your garden soon, right?"

At the time, I did not understand what this meant.

But I have gradually learned to appreciate how deeply healing spending time outside can be (Hari 2019). When I cannot go outside, I find one-on-one time with another human, or with my cats (another significant part of my support team). Light box therapy has also been useful. When I do not have enough energy for any of those, I use simulated exposure (media).

L. THERAPY, A.K.A. EMOTIONAL KNOWLEDGE

Through therapy and other sources of emotional wisdom, I have gained a pile of knowledge. Here are a few tips I like:

1. Primary caregivers being a simultaneous source of survival and care plus danger and harm is a mindfuck (M. Gilmore, interview by Frances Southwick, 2019).

2. "Revisiting the past is relevant if the past is secret, if the past is something you cannot talk about" (van der Kolk 2015).

3. Monitoring one's autonomic state is helpful for recognizing, in real time, whether a brake or accelerator needs to be employed for self-regulation, especially during therapy.[60]

4. Traumatic memories and feelings may return when one creates a safe life (Herman 1997).

5. The trajectory for healing trauma is like a spiral or loop the loop (R. Harvey, pers. comm., 2021).

6. At all times, one has the power to inflame trauma oneself through rumination. The brain must have sustenance; if it has none, it will ruminate (Magistro 2017).

7. Small exposures heal; large exposures retraumatize (K. McClure-Hunley, pers. comm., 2021).

8. An unexamined trauma may transform a victim into an abuser (D. Mortell, pers. comm., 2016).

9. A freeze response during trauma can be lifesaving at the time, and it is more likely to lead to PTSD (Herman 1997; Levine 2010; Rothschild 2000).

10. The first response from a trusted source is a critical part of the recovery process (Herman 1997).

11. One's earliest sexual exposures may inform what is sexually stimulating later in life (R. Harvey, pers. comm., 2021).

---

60 Babette Rothschild (2017) created a color-coded chart called "Autonomic Nervous System: Precision Regulation" for therapists to reference during therapy sessions. Essentially, it codes visible signs (muscle appearance, vital signs, pupils, skin tone and humidity, hand and foot temperature) with affect and autonomic states, labeled Parasympathetic I, II, and III and Sympathetic I, II, and III.

12. "Growing up being taught to ignore or numb or deny what you feel gets to be a problem because you've got to know what you feel to know what you need" (Dinneen 2021).

13. It may be an emotion, not an emergency (C. Magistro, pers. comm., 2014).

14. Estrangement is sometimes healthy and necessary (P. Ott, interview by Judith Avers, 2015).

15. "Vulnerability is the core of all emotions and feelings. To feel is to be vulnerable. To believe vulnerability is weakness is to believe that feeling is weakness. To foreclose on our emotional life out of a fear that the costs will be too high is to walk away from the very thing that gives purpose and meaning to living" (Brown 2012).

16. Emotions are not optional and must be felt, not minimized, ridiculed, avoided, or magnified, and by that token, "numb" is not an emotion (C. Poppito, pers. comm., 2015).

17. Embracing, naming, and validating emotions is a healthy way to interface with them (C. Magistro, pers. comm., 2014; C. Poppito, pers. comm., 2014; Rebekah Ballagh's "Journey to Wellness" illustrations).

18. Sharing emotions and hard experiences with others strengthens relationships (J. Avers, pers. comm., n.d.).

19. The sensation, image, behavior, affect, and meaning model, or SIBAM, is a useful paradigm to frame memories (Levine 2010).

20. Who you are is all you have (Chapman 1989).

M. MEDICATION AND SUPPLEMENTATION

Although I had terrible reactions to some medicines, medication has been useful for my symptoms related to depression, migraines, and narcolepsy with cataplexy (all of which may be entangled with c-PTSD). Daily vitamin D seems to help a little, too.

N. MUSIC AND PHYSICAL RHYTHM

Though I have not worked therapeutically with a body-psychotherapist or somatic therapist, some of my therapists have used the principles thereof, and I have read and used some of the ideas for myself. When I feel depressed or anxious, my body, and any one of my senses, can be the access point for change.

Music in particular is one of the most healing phenomena. It touches on all five points of Peter Levine's (2010) SIBAM model: sound and vibratory senses (sensation) and imagery (image), can change how one acts, whether it is snapping, drumming, swaying, or dancing (behavior); lyrics provide meaning, and all the while, affect comes along for the ride.

Here is a short piece I wrote about how in a pinch, music helps me when I dissociate:

I am paralyzed.

Muscles taut.

Tongue sewn into mandible.

Ribs squashing diaphragm.

Buttocks tucked under pelvic floor like a petrified, piddling puppy.

I am mid-exhalation.

Without warning, my neck muscles become rigid and jostle my head back and forth like a boiling tea kettle.

My arms and legs give quick gasps of movement every few seconds—

Right arm jumps.

Pause.

Left leg jumps.

Pause.

It is as if my body is receiving random electric shocks. I am the patient in the board game Operation. I await the next jolt.

"Babe?" I hear behind me. Jude is a light sleeper. I'm curled up on my right side in bed, faced away from her. It's dark in the room, but not black.

I can't answer right away, though I try. I further tighten my abdominal muscles to puff words out the top of the respiratory tract, but my jaw is rusted into place, lips glued shut.

"Babe?!" Jude is more insistent. She rolls toward me and puts her hand on my left shoulder, inducing a larger convulsion.

She knows what to do now. She rolls away and fiddles with her phone for a moment, then comes Adele.

"There's a fiiiire, starting in my heart . . . "

My abdominal muscles quiet and allow natural respiration to take over. Relief. I test my eyes—I can blink now.[61]

"And it's bringin' me out the dark . . ."

My elbow extends and shifts my weight toward Jude. I smile because I'm once again unstuck by music.

A panel of musicians, music therapists, and neurobiologists like Stephen Porges would be better at explaining why music is therapeutic. Porges dedicated an entire chapter to music in his neurobiological opus, *The Polyvagal Theory.* He writes:

> Vocalizations, in addition to facial expression, can reflect and
> trigger bodily states. Similar to the relationship between smiling

---

61 Sometimes, if played early enough, music can reverse my cataplexy.

and calmness . . . working with traumatized individuals creates a great challenge to therapists, since the normal social engagement behaviors of the therapist may trigger fear and reactive defensive strategies. Music therapy provides a special portal to reengage the social engagement system that does not require . . . face-to-face interaction. . . . Since melodic music contains acoustic properties similar to vocal prosody, music may be used to recruit the social engagement system . . . and the traumatized individual will shift to a more calm and positive physiological state. (2011)

Rhythm alone can be soothing. When people are distressed and left to themselves, they often rhythmically move themselves for reassurance.[62]

For me, music pulls together many useful elements: comfort; consistency; body engagement, especially when the rhythm is similar to my heartbeat (I *love* music with a good, thick beat); connection with another person on my terms; and control (I can stop, fast-forward, skip, repeat, or rewind anytime). Plus I can put a cork in my vulnerability, which is a powerful and important part of treatment, but it can be draining and counterproductive if used continuously.

Of course, I also enjoy the *meaning* and witnessed experience from lyrics. It is like having permission and direction for projected identification with the option to feel it myself. Autobiographical musicians like Ani DiFranco, Aimee Mann, Judith Avers, Frazey Ford, and Karen Savoca produce material I find particularly therapeutic. I also use certain trance-like beats with wise words, such as those in Jose Gonzales's album *Vestiges & Claws*, for comfort and relaxation.

---

62 A word of caution—rhythmic behaviors, when protracted and associated with marked changes in cognition (e.g., metronome-like rocking, pacing or rocking that cannot be interrupted), can signify severe distress or pathology (Navarro 2014; Grandin and Johnson 2009).

Beatboxing and drumming have also been a big help to me (especially beatboxing because my instrument is always with me.)

APPENDIX F: MY PERSONAL MAINTENANCE PLAN

My recovery is a sine wave of high and low notes, gradually oscillating to a more and more consistent tone. As so many trauma therapists emphasize, healing from trauma is a lifelong process. Letting go of the adage "get over it" is difficult because it is so culturally embedded. But accepting the trauma as part of my life experience, allowing myself to use it, and finding ways to "carry the pain in a different way," as Dr. Dolcetti says, is helpful in my process. For me, recovery is not about eclipse, but integration. Here are some of the main techniques I employ for maintenance. Some sources are mentioned, but many more have supported these techniques.

1. Cherish (give and receive love and support in) my healthy relationships (Hari 2019).

2. Uphold the boundaries I create (Shetty 2020).

3. Play music and drink tea when I am alone (Sacks 1985).

4. Walk outside each weekend with a loved one (Hari 2019).

5. Write and draw (Pennebaker 2004).

6. Keep a wheel of emotions in my backpack and on the fridge (Plutchik and Kellerman 1980).

7. Take my medicine daily, using a pill box and alarm (Armstrong 2011).

8. Talk to my trusted confidantes when I am feeling low (Hari 2019).

9. Stop and pet the California poppies on my walks (Hari 2019; J. Avers, pers. comm., n.d.).

10. Take trips to sit on the beach and to walk in the California redwoods (Hari 2019).

11. Work. My work is part of who I am.

APPENDIX G: PHYSICAL APPROACHES TO TREATMENT OF POST-TRAUMATIC SYNDROMES

"Simply touching an injured area can trigger a serious emotional reaction. Some might say that the area touched merely acts as a trigger by sending proprioceptive stimuli to the central nerves. . . .
The tissue itself can serve as an "emotional warehouse."

—Jean-Pierre Barral and Alain Croibier, *Trauma: An Osteopathic Approach*

In my own experience as a person living with PTSD, hands-off physical engagement, such as stretching, yoga, tai chi, walking, drumming, and certain breathing exercises, have yielded some benefit related to my symptoms. I have also experienced positive responses from hands-on treatment, including massage, physical therapy (including pelvic floor physical therapy), osteopathic manipulative treatment (OMT), and acupuncture. The treatments that produce positive responses seem to have the following things in common:

1.   Consistency and a low-stimulation environment

2.   Healthy physical and psychic boundaries of the practitioner (mostly nonverbally communicated)

3.   Humility of the practitioner

4.   Strong knowledge base of the practitioner

However, an abundance of consideration and caution is necessary when planning how to engage with and treat those with post-traumatic syndromes. When it comes to manual (hands-on) approaches, because physical engagement with another human involves close proximity and adds layers of stimulation, there is more potential for significant retraumatization than with indirect treatment. Even when receiving care from seasoned practitioners in massage, structural integration, and OMT, I have had memorably negative responses, even in cases in which I self-disclosed my PTSD diagnosis. These negative responses seemed to have basis in one or more of the following complications:

1.   Weak knowledge base of the practitioner, despite good intention

2.   Lack of appropriate physical or psychic boundaries of the practitioner, despite good intention

3.   An unbalanced degree of confidence, humility, and/or empathy of the practitioner

4.   Overly rushed treatment or a stimulating treatment environment

Though beyond the scope of this book, many physical approaches can be helpful in stabilizing and normalizing neural tone, thereby reducing reactivity and improving symptoms related to PTSD. That said, because I am a DO, I would be remiss to not comment specifically on OMT.[63]

---

63 Regarding studies on OMT's efficacy, I find it helpful to keep in mind that randomized, double-blind studies are not possible because the provider will always know whether they are performing OMT.

Patients present with a variety of complaints. As an osteopathic physician, after taking a standard medical history, I may perform an osteopathic history and physical examination. When somatic dysfunction (impaired or altered function of the components of the somatic system [skeletal, arthrodial, and myofascial structures and related vascular, lymphatic, and neural elements]) is found, I can offer OMT. OMT involves the hands of the practitioner on the body of the person with the complaint. The goal is nonjudgmental observation of tissue texture and motion, and encouragement of the tissue to a more functional structure and motion pattern. It can be as gentle as Reiki or as forceful as a stereotypical chiropractic adjustment.

PTSD's embeddedness in the autonomic nervous system and association with multiple predictable somatic complaints leads me to believe that OMT could be useful for somatic dysfunction secondary to PTSD. However, I have not performed OMT specifically for PTSD; then again, I also have not performed OMT for back pain or headache. In general, osteopathic manipulation is not applied to allopathic diagnoses via a treatment algorithm; it is applied based on patient history and osteopathic evaluation.

Osteopathic providers know that prescriptive treatment or segmental evaluation is not holistic. However, somatic patterns emerge in various states of disease. When an individual displays central nervous system irritability or dysregulation, especially of the autonomic nervous system, particular attention should be placed on evaluating the individual for somatic dysfunction in the head, cervical spine, thoracic spine, abdominal diaphragm, ribs, sacrum, and iliopsoas. The choice of a particular treatment, including CV4, muscle energy at the occipitoatlantal (OA) joint, myofascial release or muscle energy of the trapezius and cervicothoracic (CT) junction, doming of the abdominal diaphragm, rib raising, and sacral treatment, depends on examination findings and clinical judgment (Alphonso 2020).

APPENDIX H:
NARCOLEPSY WITH CATAPLEXY

Marsha Linehan, renowned psychologist and creator of dialectical behavioral therapy (DBT) was hospitalized as a teen for suicidal behavior. In a note to her psychiatrist, she mentioned falling down:

My veneer is pretty good at the moment but I am depressed about your statement as to how long I may be here. I talked to both my parents & got that straightened out. I am so mixed up as to how I feel. My bottom coat is so depressed, dejected, discouraged, hopeless & unhappy but my top coat keeps smiling. I feel like smashing, biting, breaking & ramming into something. I feel guilty about falling (did again) because I can't get over the feeling that I am doing it on purpose. Am I? I feel terrible, terrible, terrible but can't do anything about it. (2020)

I cannot be sure, but I believe Linehan experienced cataplexy. Cataplexy can be experienced independently, but it can also be part of a larger syndrome called type 1 narcolepsy, which I live with. Type 1 narcolepsy, also known as narcolepsy with cataplexy, is a neurodegenerative autoimmune disease that destroys hypocretin-secreting cells in the hypothalamus.

Cataplexy presents as mild to severe weakness of the body. If I have not eaten or slept well recently, it can present as a complete physical collapse with no control of any voluntary muscle, and it can sometimes even make breathing difficult. It is as if my parasympathetic nervous system overrides all other functioning to the point of collapse. These episodes occur when I am emotionally overwhelmed.

After about twenty to forty minutes of weakness come sighs reminiscent of the social engagement Stanley Rosenberg describes as the indication of successful "Basic Exercise" application (2017), then stretches, then trembling. Some authors describe trembling as part of the immediate recovery after a traumatic event (Levine 2010).

I have collapsed due to cataplexy on numerous occasions, including when I first told Jude I loved her, when I was triggered as a pre-teen at a Christian summer camp by a fellow camper who poured her heart out at our campfire about her recent rape, when I was delivering a speech, when I learned the verdict of the trial, and many other times. With conservative measures and medication, I now experience mild to moderate cataplexy approximately every other week.

The association between trauma and type 1 narcolepsy is an area that warrants further study.

APPENDIX I: C-PTSD CRITERIA

Autonomic dysregulation could be added to the c-PTSD criteria created by Judith Herman, as follows:[64]

Alterations in autonomic regulation, including involuntary, rapid, and/or distressing fluctuations among six sensate and observable autonomic states:

Lethargy (Parasympathetic I), characterized by apathy and depression, associated with grief, sadness, shame, disgust, and withdrawal from others

Calm (Parasympathetic II), the state of social engagement characterized by feelings of safety, pleasure, clear thinking, and relaxation

Active/Alert (Sympathetic I), an alert state characterized by a readiness to act with a moderate level of arousal

Flight/Fight (Sympathetic II), a normal reaction to danger characterized by a rapid heart rate; dry, cold hands and feet; rage; and fear

Hyper-freeze (Sympathetic III), a state of overload, known colloquially as "deer in headlights," characterized by terror and dissociation

Hypo-freeze (Parasympathetic III), a state in preparation for death, also known as dorsal vagal collapse

---

64 This proposed addition to the definition of c-PTSD is informed by the works of Stephen Porges (2011) and Babette Rothschild (2017).

APPENDIX J: PATIENT FORMS

I wrote Patient Forms A, B, and C for my patients. These practical handouts were designed to infuse trauma-informed care into a busy office setting, as there is not always time to talk in detail about essential health maintenance.

Permission is granted for behavioral health and medical use. Please credit F. Southwick on copies when distributing or reproducing.

Patient Form A: I give the "Self-Interview" form to new patients, patients who screen positive on the Generalized Anxiety Disorder-2 (GAD-2) or Patient Health Questionnaire-2 (PHQ-2) screenings, patients who decline or are unable to access psychotherapy, and any adult as a general wellness tool. It is appropriate for anyone thirteen years of age or older with a third grade reading level or higher.

Thank you to Ani DiFranco (2021), Viktor Frankl (1984), Johann Hari (2019), and Bessel van der Kolk and Ruth Buczynski (n.d.), whose research and writings informed the content and structure of this form.

Patient Form B: At well-child visits I give the "Dear Young Patient" letter to kids between ten and eighteen years of age with a fourth grade reading level or higher. This is my contribution to the larger goal of creating a "saner society." It is effectively an abridged children's bill of rights (Bloom 2013; Robinson 2020).

Patient Form C: I give the "Dear Kind Patient" letter to new adult patients with a fifth grade reading level or higher.

Thank you to Stephen Porges (2011) and Christian Robinson (2020), whose research and writings informed the content and structure of this letter.

PATIENT FORM A: SELF-INTERVIEW

Self-Interview

Name and birthday: Date:

1. Who do you feel good being around?

2. Who do you feel good talking with on the phone?

3. What group do you feel good to be a part of?

4. Whose life has been (even a tiny little bit) better because of you?

5. After having hard times, some people become really sensitive and in tune with other peoples' feelings. Do you think this applies to you?

6. Some people go on walks or have a plant or pet. How do you spend time with nature?

7. What do you do to move your body?

8. Think about today. Can you name one thought that brought on each of the following feelings?

    a. Mad   c. Sad   e. Excited

    b. Scared   d. Relaxed

9. When they feel lonely but can't or don't want to connect with anyone, some people do things such as close their eyes and breathe, read a book, look at the sky, or watch shows. If you can't reach another human, how do you soothe your natural loneliness?

10. Basic needs are food, sleep, water, shelter, interactions with others, good hygiene, and good health. What basic needs are you meeting for yourself?

11. Think of a moment you felt good on a really deep level, and say what it was.

12. "Bad" feelings (pain, sadness, fear) are really helpful because they are trying to protect us, or help us understand what is happening. What helpful things do you think your "bad" feelings are trying to tell you?

13. Some people like to drum, whistle, sing, dance, snap, or clap. Even the heart beats with rhythm. Name one way you make a rhythm.

PATIENT FORM B: DEAR YOUNG PATIENT

Dear Young Patient,

Thank you for coming in today. This is a note to tell you your rights and give you a few tips about your medical health.

1. The medical providers here (including me) are trustworthy adults. You can talk with us about your worries, stresses, and injuries. You can ask us questions about your body, puberty, sex, and anything else you can dream up. Consider us a resource as you grow up.

2. No one has the right to hurt you.

3. No one has the right to touch you on any body part.

4. No one has the right to make you see or do things you are uncomfortable with. If you aren't sure about something, talk to your trusted adults.

5. You should never make someone else do something they don't want to do or see something they don't want to see. Anytime you touch someone else, you need to ask if it's okay first. That is called consent.

6.   No secrets should be kept from your caregivers. If you don't feel comfortable sharing something with your caregivers, then talk with a medical provider or other trusted adult.

We will see you every year for a check-up. I'm glad you are doing so well—I will see you at your next visit.

Until then, please brush your teeth twice a day, and remember: **You Matter**.

In kindness,

PATIENT FORM C: DEAR KIND PATIENT

Dear Kind Patient,

Being a person is hard work.

There is so much to do.

Sleep well for seven to eight hours nightly.

Mostly eat real foods (fruits, veggies, nuts, seeds, beans, as well as milk and lean meats, such as fish, poultry, and chicken, if you aren't vegan).

Use healthy coping skills, such as walking, drawing, and connecting with loved ones.

Get forty minutes of exercise four days a week.

Choose healthy relationships.

Use good posture while sitting, standing, and sleeping.

Drink enough clean water.

Brush your teeth twice daily.

Limit toxic stress, or stress that is severe enough to make someone want to give up or die.

Avoid pollutants and unnecessary chemicals.

Get enough fresh air.

Recognize, accept, and work with the stresses and traumas of childhood and previous relationships.

Use a pill box to take your medicine every day.

Find at least a minute of time every day to be quiet.

WHOA! That is a LOT.

Punishing oneself is a common response when reading the items on this list. Some people think, "I'm terrible at all these things," or "I'll never be able to do it all, so why bother?"

My recommendation as your medical provider is to *take it easy on yourself*. Remember, you are human, and you have human limits. You can make changes. They will take time. The more you rail against yourself for your self-perceived shortcomings, the harder it will be to get where you want to be. In other words, what you resist, persists. I will do my best to help us both remember this.

Once we let go of self-judgement *just a little bit*, we have room for self-love and feeling better. And by "feeling better," I mean slow, gentle change . . . one thing at a time.

Just by reading this letter, you have done something really good for yourself.

I am proud of you for reaching out. And remember: **You Matter**.

In kindness,

BIBLIOGRAPHY

Alphonso, H. M. "Psychiatry and OMM/OMT." Convocation speech, American Academy of Osteopathy, March 21, 2020.

American Psychiatric Association. *Diagnostic and Statistical Manual of Mental Disorders*. 5th ed. Washington DC: American Psychiatric Association, 2013.

Annibale, Brooke, vocalist. "Patience." *The Simple Fear*. Brooke Annibale, 2015, CD-ROM.

Armstrong, Carrie. "APA Releases Guideline on Treatment of Patients with Major Depressive Disorder." *American Family Physician* 83, no. 10 (May 15, 2011): 1219-1227.

Association for the Treatment of Sexual Abusers. "Children with Sexual Behavior Problems." N.d. Accessed November 15, 2016. http://www.atsa.com/children-sexual-behavior-problems

Bareja, Pawan. "4 Ways to Heal Yourself with Love." *Lion's Roar*, Janurary 28, 2021.

Barral, Jean-Pierre, and Alain Croibier. *Trauma: An Osteopathic Approach*. Seattle: Eastland Press, 1999.

Bedi, Saaniya, Elliot C. Nelson, Michael T. Lynskey, Vivia V. McCutcheon, Andrew C. Heath, Pamela A. Madden, and Nicholas G. Martin. "Risk for Suicidal Thoughts and Behavior After Childhood Sexual Abuse in Women and Men." *Suicide and Life Threatening Behavior* 41, no. 4 (August 2011): 406-415. doi: 10.1111/j.1943-278X.2011.00040.x

Bloom, Sandra L. *Creating Sanctuary: Toward the Evolution of Sane Societies*. New York: Taylor & Francis, 2013.

Brach, Tara. "The Healing Journey: Rosalie's Story." *Lion's Roar*, January 28, 2021.

Brown, Brené. *Daring Greatly: How the Courage to Be Vulnerable Transforms the Way We Live, Love, Parent, and Lead.* New York: Penguin, 2012.

Brown, Brené. *The Gifts of Imperfection: Let Go of Who You Think You're Supposed to Be and Embrace Who You Are.* Center City: Hazelden Publishing, 2010.

Centers for Disease Control and Prevention. "Infographic: 6 Guiding Principles To a Trauma-Informed Approach." Last modified September 17, 2020. https://www.cdc.gov/cpr/infographics/6_principles_trauma_info.htm

Centers for Disease Control and Prevention. "Leading Causes of Death and Injury." Last modified Februrary 11, 2021. https://www.cdc.gov/injury/wisqars/LeadingCauses.html

Chapman, Tracy, vocalist. "All That You Have Is Your Soul." *Crossroads.* Tracy Chapman, 1989, CD-ROM.

Csanyi, Carolyn. "Homemade Grafting Wax." *SFGATE*, n.d. Accessed July 30, 2021. https://homeguides.sfgate.com/homemade-grafting-wax-85417.html

Cuddy, Amy. "Your Body Language May Shape Who You Are." Filmed June 2012. TED video, 20:46. https://www.ted.com/talks/amy_cuddy_your_body_language_may_shape_who_you_are?language=en

Damasio, Antonio. *Descartes' Error: Emotion, Reason, and the Human Brain.* New York: Penguin, 2005.

DiFranco, Ani, vocalist. "Revolutionary Love." *Revolutionary Love.* Ani DiFranco, 2021, CD-ROM.

Dinneen, Allyson. *Notes from Your Therapist.* Boston: Houghton Mifflin Harcourt, 2021.

Division of Violence Prevention, National Center for Injury Prevention and Control, Centers for Disease Control and Prevention. "Preventing Adverse Childhood Experiences (ACEs): Leveraging the Best Available Evidence." PDF file, Atlanta, 2019. https://www.cdc.gov/violenceprevention/pdf/preventingACES.pdf

Dubowitz, Howard, Susan Feigelman, Wendy Lane, and Jeongeun Kim. "Pediatric Primary Care to Help Prevent Child Maltreatment: The Safe Environment for Every Kid (SEEK) Model." Pediatrics 123, no. 3 (March 2009): 858-864. doi: 10.1542/peds.2008-1376

Felliti, V. J., R. F. Anda, D. Nordenberg, D. F. Williamson, A. M. Spitz, V. Edwards, M. P. Koss, and J. S. Marks. "Relationship of Childhood Abuse and Household Dysfunction to Many of the Leading Causes of Death in Adults. The Adverse Childhood Experiences (ACE) Study." American Journal of Preventive Medicine 14, no. 4 (May 1998): 245-258. doi: 10.1016/s0749-3797(98)00017-8

Frankl, Viktor. Man's Search for Meaning. Boston: Pocket Books of Simon and Schuster, Inc., 1984.

Gorman, Amanda. "The Miracle of Morning." PBS, January 21, 2021. https://www.pbs.org/newshour/arts/amanda-gormans-poetic-answer-to-pandemic-grief-do-not-ignore-the-pain

Gottlieb, Lori. Maybe You Should Talk to Someone: A Therapist, HER Therapist, and Our Lives Revealed. Boston: Houghton Mifflin Harcourt, 2019.

Gramlich, John. "What the Data Says (And Doesn't Say) About Crime in the United States." Pew Research Center, November 20, 2020. https://www.pewresearch.org/fact-tank/2020/11/20/facts-about-crime-in-the-u-s/

Grandin, Temple, and Catherine Johnson. Animals Make Us Human: Creating the Best Life for Animals. New York: First Mariner, 2009.

Hari, Johann. "This Could be Why You're Depressed or Anxious." Filmed July 2019. TED video, 20:23. https://www.ted.com/talks/johann_hari_this_could_be_why_you_re_depressed_or_anxious?language=en

Hein, Denise, Lisa Caren Litt, Lisa R. Cohen, Gloria M. Miele, and Aimee Campbell. Trauma Services for Women in Substance Abuse Treatment: An Integrated Approach. Washington DC: American Psychological Association, 2009.

Herman, Judith. Trauma and Recovery: The Aftermath of Violence—From Domestic Abuse to Political Terror. New York: Basic Books, 1997.

Johnson, T. "Child Perpetrators – Children who Molest Other Children: Preliminary Findings." Child Abuse and Neglect 12, no. 2 (1988): 219-229. doi: 10.1016/0145-2134(88)90030-0

Kellogg, Nancy D. "Sexual Behaviors in Children: Evaluation and Management." American Family Physician 82 no. 10 (November 2010): 1233-1238.

Kuchera, Michael L., and William A. Kuchera. Osteopathic Considerations in Systemic Dysfunction. 2nd ed. Columbus: Greyden, 1994.

Levine, Peter. In An Unspoken Voice: How the Body Releases Trauma and Restores Goodness. Berkeley: North Atlantic, 2010.

Linehan, Marsha. Building A Life Worth Living. New York: Random House, 2020.

Linehan, Marsha, Kelly McGonigal, Ron Siegel, Joan Borysenko, and Bill O'Hanlon. "How to Break the Power of Shame by Engaging It." How to Work with Shame. Program from the National Institute for the Clinical Application of Behavioral Medicine, May 2, 2021.

Loewenstein, Richard J. "Dissociation Debates: Everything You Know is Wrong." Dialogues in Clinical Neuroscience 20, no. 3 (September 2018): 229-242. doi: 10.31887/DCNS.2018.20.3/rloewenstein

Lowry, Lois. The Giver. New York: Random House, 1993.

Magistro, Cynthia. "Think Less. Feel More." Cynthia Magistro, July 6, 2017.

Miller, Jean Baker. Toward a New Psychology of Women. Boston: Beacon, 1986.

Morabito, Melissa S., Linda M. Williams, and April Pattavina. "Decision Making in Sexual Assault Cases: Replication Research on Sexual Violence Case Attrition in the U.S." PDF file, February 2019. https://www.ojp.gov/pdffiles1/nij/grants/252689.pdf

Morrison, Toni. Beloved. New York: Alfred A. Knopf, Inc., 1987.

Morrison, Toni. God Help the Child. New York: Alfred A. Knopf, Inc., 2015.

Morrison, Toni. Home. New York: Alfred A. Knopf, Inc., 2012.

Morrison, Toni. Jazz. New York: Alfred A. Knopf, Inc., 1992.

Morrison, Toni. Love. New York: Alfred A. Knopf, Inc., 2003.

Morrison, Toni. Sula. New York: Alfred A. Knopf, Inc., 1973.

Morrison, Toni. Tar Baby. New York: Alfred A. Knopf, Inc., 1981.

Nappi, Carla M., Sean P. A. Drummond, and Joshua M. H. Hall. "Treating Nightmares and Insomnia in Posttraumatic Stress Disorder: A Review of Current Evidence." Neuropharmacology 62, no. 2 (February 2012): 576-585. doi: 10.1016/j.neuropharm.2011.02.029

National Institute of Neurological Disorders and Stroke. "Traumatic Brain Injury Information Page." Last modified March 27, 2019. https://www.ninds.nih.gov/Disorders/All-Disorders/Traumatic-Brain-Injury-Information-Page

Navarro, Joe. "5 Ways That Body Language Can Signal Trouble." Psychology Today, January 1, 2014. https://www.psychologytoday.com/us/blog/spycatcher/201401/5-ways-body-language-can-signal-trouble

Newton, Isaac. Philosophiae Naturalis Principia Mathematica. London: Royal Society, 1686.

Ogilvie, Beverly A. Mother-Daughter Incest. Binghamton: Haworth Press, Inc., 2004.

Ontario Neurotrauma Foundation. "Clinical Practice Guideline for the Rehabilitation of Adults with Moderate to Severe TBI." October 2016. https://braininjuryguidelines.org/modtosevere/

Oprah.com. "The Oprah Winfrey Show Finale." March 25, 2011. http://www.oprah.com/oprahshow/the-oprah-winfrey-show-finale_1/9

Pennebaker, James W. Writing to Heal: A Guided Journal for Recovering from Trauma & Emotional Upheaval. Oakland: New Harbinger, 2004.

Pert, Candace B. Molecules of Emotion: Why You Feel the Way You Feel. New York: Scribner, 1997.

Plutchik, Robert, and Henry Kellerman. Emotion: Theory, Research, and Experience, Volume 1: Theories of Emotion. New York: Academic Press, 1980.

Porges, Stephen. The Polyvagal Theory: Neurophysiological Foundations of Emotions, Attachment, Communication, and Self-regulation. New York: W. W. Norton & Co., 2011.

Rape, Abuse & Incest National Network. "Child Sexual Abuse." N.d. Accessed May 7, 2021. https://www.rainn.org/articles/child-sexual-abuse

Rape Crisis – Cape Town Trust. "Rape Trauma Syndrome (RTS)." N.d. Accessed August 23, 2015. http://rapecrisis.org.za/information-for-survivors/rape-trauma-syndrome/

Razak, Arisika. "The Trauma of an American Untouchable." Lion's Roar, March 5, 2021.

Robinson, Christian. You Matter. New York: Atheneum, Simon and Schuster, 2020.

Rosenberg, Stanley. Accessing the Healing Power of the Vagus Nerve. Berkeley: North Atlantic Books, 2017.

Rothschild, Babette. The Body Remembers: The Psychophysiology of Trauma and Trauma Treatment. New York: W. W. Norton & Co., 2000.

Rothschild, Babette. The Body Remembers Volume 2: Revolutionizing Trauma Treatment. New York: W. W. Norton & Co., 2017.

Sacks, Oliver. The Man Who Mistook His Wife for a Hat. New York, London: Summit Books, Gerald Duckworth and Co., Ltd., 1985.

SEEK. "Parent Questionnaire - R." PDF file, 2019. https://seekwellbeing.org/wp-content/uploads/2019/09/English_PQ-R.pdf

Shetty, Jay (@jayshetty). "Leave a 'YES' below if you agree. If you're blessed enough to have removed a toxic person from your life, don't try and bring that negativity back in. Quote: @realtalkkim." Instagram photo, November 20, 2020. https://www.instagram.com/p/CH0qdhilhU8/

Still, A. T. Philosophy of Osteopathy. Kirksville: A. T. Still, 1899.

University of California. "Plum Rootstock & Scion Selection." N.d. Accessed June 13, 2021. http://fruitandnuteducation.ucdavis.edu/fruitnutproduction/Plum/Plum_scion_root/

Van der Kolk, Bessel. "The Body Keeps the Score: Brain, Mind, and Body in the Healing of Trauma." May 22, 2015. YouTube video, 1:40:27. https://www.youtube.com/watch?app=desktop&v=53RX2ESIqsM

Van der Kolk, Bessel. The Body Keeps the Score: Brain, Mind, and Body in the Healing of Trauma. New York: Penguin, 2015.

Van der Kolk, Bessel, and Bill O'Hanlon. "How to Work With Shame When It's Connected to Trauma. Part 1: A Way to Heal Trauma-Based Shame Using a 3-Dimensional Space." How to Work with Shame. Program from the National Institute for the Clinical Application of Behavioral Medicine, May 3, 2021.